Personally Branded

The Smart Way to Showcase Yourself
at Work and Socially

Sheri Fermanich

Copyright © 2013 Sheri Fermanich
All rights reserved.

ISBN: 1480085715
ISBN-13: 978-1480085718

Table of Contents

Street Smart Lesson 1	Sell It Like a Brand	1
Street Smart Lesson 2	What Makes a Personal Brand Great?	23
Street Smart Lesson 3	Brand YOU Rules and Authenticity	41
Street Smart Lesson 4	Brand YOU Foundation	67
Street Smart Lesson 5	Brand Management	99
Street Smart Lesson 6	If You Don't Brand Yourself	117
Street Smart Lesson 7	Courageously Live Brand YOU	133

Introduction

The need to showcase your best talents and abilities at work has been around for ages. When someone wants to be noticed at work or considered for a major project, they do their best, often with very little training in regard to self-promotion. The age-old idea of competition is usually the attempted approach. However, "nice girls" might even fall into the trap that is it not polite to call attention to yourself and your expertise.

It is no longer necessary to use these old and often ineffective means to stand out in our professional and personal life. The biggest problem with that style of thinking is that it is false competition. You are the only true competition that you will ever have. You will never have exactly the same skills, ability, style, and expertise as anyone else. It is foolish to pretend that is the situation.

Personal branding has been around since the 1990s. In the beginning it was used primarily for entrepreneurs and high-level executives to gain business. Today virtually everyone could benefit from knowing how to use personal branding.

There are so many uses for personal branding. As you read through *Personally Branded* you will gain valuable information and learn critical things about yourself that will help you tremendously.

You might as well know a secret up front. You already have a brand whether you are aware of it or not. I am sure that you agree it is far better to take control of your brand than find yourself accidentally branded.

Personally Branded is written for people who work for an employer and do not have to do their own actual advertising. If you are an entrepreneur or independent salesperson, the Priceless Asset$ A Step-by-Step Guide to Personal Branding success system located at StreetSmartPublishing.com is the correct product for you.

The exciting part about being personally branded is that you have the potential to stand out and prosper in the world. If your mission is to be your best self and do your best work, you can make an amazing impact.

With *Personally Branded* you will learn to honor your unique talents and build your skills. Doing this work will enable you to create an authentic brand that you can be truly proud of.

Can *Personally* Branded help you?

Are you an employee who wants a promotion?
Do you work for a company where you have to make sure you get noticed?
Do you participate in any networking events?
Do you want a certain image in your community?
Do you want recognition and rewards?

Introduction

Do you realize you are capable of gaining more rewards? If so, do you know how to make that happen?
Are you in an industry where there is strong competition?
Do you have a certain reputation that needs changing?

If you answered yes to any of these questions, *Personally Branded* will be worth multiple times its purchase price.

Quite frankly, you can also use personal branding in your private life as a parent, spouse, neighbor, or community volunteer. Simply adjust how and what you are doing to communicate your brand personally.

We all know how to do this in the dating sense. Think about it. If you want to date a particular person then you probably want them to perceive you in a certain way. You carry this image over into how you talk, act, dress, and interact with the potential date. You orchestrate a personal campaign to show this person how great you are and that you are the one for them! You do not need to play games. The direct approach is often the approach that works.

Our entire focus and purpose here will be a general understanding of personal branding and how to showcase who you are in a smart way.

STREET SMART LESSON 1

Sell It Like a Brand

You have amazing talents that need to be shared with others. Have you ever thought about that? You have an obligation to share your unique gifts with the world. What if no one felt like sharing his or her talents in the marketplace?

It's time to step up and not fear being you in the world. No more hiding! There is no room in personal branding for you to sell out. Personal branding is a bold, passionate, courageous, respectful expression of yourself and what you have to offer. You owe it to yourself and to those who could benefit from what you have to offer to dynamically show that what you have to offer is of value.

I am going to show you how to take who you are, what you have to offer and turn it into a **personal brand**. There is nothing random about personal branding. Personal branding is strategic. When you use personal branding you take control of how people perceive you. You manage the process through marketing to help you achieve your goals.

Some books will tell you that personal branding is how you dress when you show up at a networking event. This has caused confusion about what personal branding is really about. Personal branding is *not* solely your physical image. That is just one component.

Personal Branding (verb): a strategic process of marketing people and their careers as a brand. Personal branding controls the perception the marketplace has of:

1) Who you are.
2) What you do.
3) Your unique selling proposition (differentiation).
4) How you benefit your target audience.

Personal branding is an ongoing activity that can be fun. There are five steps to personal branding:

1) Understand yourself.
2) Understand the process of personal branding.
3) Create your personal brand.
4) Implement your personal brand.
5) Continually evaluate and improve your personal brand.

I will show you all five steps throughout this book. You can go as quickly or slowly through each lesson as you like. That is the great thing about street smart learning. It lets you get what you need, how and when you need it. Let's get started with branding in general.

What's Branding?

I am sure you are familiar with corporate brands such as Nike, Coca Cola and Porsche. Many people think a brand is just the name of a product. The brand is more than the name. It is a feeling that the company wants you to have when you think of their product. Here are three examples:

- Disney–the happiest place on earth
- FedEx–reliability
- Tiger Woods–excellence

These companies spend years and millions of dollars defining and promoting these brands in the marketplace. In the last twenty years branding has become a big business. In some cases the brand itself is worth more than the physical product. The name "Martha Stewart" is insured for what might seem like an excessive amount of money because it is the essence of the brand.

Uniqueness in marketing is very important when it comes to the consumer. If a buyer thinks there is no difference between my brand and the next, he or she will just grab whichever product happens to be most accessible. Businesses do not want buyers doing that. They want loyal customers who stick with their brands no matter where they are buying them.

A great example of branding is comparing two cola products. How would you describe Pepsi? Is it harsh, sweet, salty, bland? Take note of anything you can think of including the packaging. Now do the same for Coca Cola. Is it harsh, sweet, salty, bland? What is the Coca Cola packing like?

Most consumers think Pepsi and Coke are very different. Pepsi is branded as a sweeter, all American, more broadly appealing, refreshing soft drink. Coca Cola on the other hand is a strong, bold, harsh, experience drink. When you have had a Coke, you know it.

When someone orders a cola in a restaurant and is told their preferred brand isn't offered, they may switch to a different drink altogether. This is exactly what these companies want–loyal brand users.

Companies work really hard and spend large amounts of money on establishing a winning brand. It is usually risky to change your brand once you have worked out a winning formula. Coca Cola is an example of this. In the '90s they changed the traditional formula for Coca Cola. Ninety days and millions of dollars later they changed back to the original formula because the consumer rejected the "New Coke."

When it comes to personal brands that is not always true. It depends on the industry you work in. Celebrities' brands are more acceptable, and often expected to change and evolve to keep our attention. Employees, on the other hand, need to be more careful about a brand change.

We are all familiar with celebrities creating their own "brand." Madonna is famous for re-inventing her brand every few years. She was incredibly smart to realize right away that she had to keep evolving to keep us interested and buying more products. In the early years she used shock value to keep us talking about her. Once she became a mother she switched to more subdued characters (remember her cowboy outfit and the 1950's motherly look?). Now she's on to world issues. Like her or not, she has been brilliant at keeping consumers interested and buying her brand.

Some people seem to naturally have a brand. The heavy muscles and Mohawk of former actor and bodyguard Mr. T make him an unlikely candidate to play a nanny. He is more credible as the tough guy. Bill Gates does not come to mind first as a ruthless businessman. The Bill and Melinda Gates Foundation gives you a clue as to what his brand is really about.

When you think of Paris Hilton, an image quickly forms in your mind. She is famous for being famous. She has proven to be very smart at creating a buzz about herself and profiting enormously from her branding. When you break her brand down she is a pretty female with wealthy parents, who likes to entertain people by partying. That type of brand doesn't work for everyone. After a jail sentence for drunk driving in 2007 her brand was not working for her. After emerging from her jail sentence, Paris tried to appear prim and proper with a new concern for world issues. However, this brand did not last long. She was soon back to partying as her main branding style. Her grandfather strongly opposed her brand which cost her millions of dollars when she was cut out of her grandfather's will.

What we learn by comparing Madonna and Paris Hilton is that we have to proactively control our own brands.

In reality, we all have a personal brand whether we are aware of it or not. The problem is that most people do not realize this and miss out on the benefits that branding could bring them.

Why Would You Need Personal Branding?

Personal branding is not just for celebrities and big businesses. It has become a necessity today for employees, coaches, community leaders, volunteers, etc. Let me show you why. Let's say that you get a letter from your health care provider stating that your favorite doctor is leaving your clinic. They proceed to tell you that you will need to pick a new doctor from the list below; all from internal medicine, by a specific date and let them know.

- Addison, Joan F., MD, FACP
- Hall, George M., MD MS
- Jensen, Mark, MD
- White, Jennifer J., MD

Who would you choose? Exactly. You can't decide because you know nothing about them and what they can offer you or if you'll like them. Let's say you work in a company with 300 employees. Who's Amanda Brown in Accounting? You probably would not know unless she has branded herself "the ultimate problem solver." This is why personal branding has become essential. You need to be able to stand out, get noticed and reach your goals. It's not arrogance. It's a necessity.

Who Were You Meant To Be?

To help you identify the best Brand YOU possible, think back to when you were a little kid dreaming of who you would be one day. With great passion you imagined being a dancer, a firefighter, a teacher, or a star. Each dream seemed so real and you believed with all your heart that absolutely anything was possible.

How you felt as a kid was probably more accurate in terms of who your spirit was meant to be than your perceptions today. You had no inhibitions at that young age. Your natural likes, dislikes, style and personality were honest and not affected by society. Granted, they were certainly in rough form, meaning they needed to develop and refine over time, but the essence of you are was already there.

- Who did you want to be when you were five years old?
- Who was your favorite role model growing up?
- What did you think was cool about them?

That magic didn't go away. As an adult you just decided to get more serious and maybe even a little cynical. You forgot your imagination and that anything is possible if you try hard enough. Let yourself remember what you use to be like.

BRAND-STORM: What were you like in middle school?

Think about yourself as you grew up. In middle school, how would you describe yourself? What did you like? What "group" were you a part of? Write down a few notes that may help you later in working your brand.

_____

_____

_____

_____

BRAND-STORM: What were you like in high school?

In high school, as your personality developed, what interested you the most?
What were you known for? What were you good at? What were you bad at?

_____

_____

_____

Sadly, some of us do not feel the best about ourselves now. Or maybe we grew in a positive way as we matured. The exciting part is that we can change if we are ready to play again and redefine who we really want to be in this world.

Isolating Your Personal Brand

You may think that regular people (non-celebrities) create, invent, or dream up a personal brand that is all smoke and mirrors. I can guarantee you that if you know someone like that it won't last because it's not real. This is absolutely the wrong way to go about branding. False branding will feel false to you and eventually the people you work with.

Your brand will be the right fit for you if it feels comfortable the majority of the time. It will also be a flawless transition between your personal and professional lives.

One of the best ways to do this is to isolate your core values and use them as the foundation of your personal brand. This will ensure that your personal brand will reflect who you really are.

I'm going to limit you to picking the three MOST IMPORTANT values to focus on (even though you'll start with a longer brainstormed list). Why? Because it forces you to really prioritize.

Remember the old "stranded on a desert island" assignment from school? You needed to decide the top three items or the one person whom you would take with you. It made you think through a lot of things. Your choices reflected your real priorities. As an example, I will share with you my top three values.

- Family
- Freedom
- Growth

Three simple words, but they are the foundation on which I build my entire life.

1) FAMILY My family of origin had a major effect on me. My mom, sister and I are extremely close. The three of us made it through each life adventure with unconditional support and encouragement for each other.

I was one of those kids who wanted to be a mom since I was little. I have the great fortune to be married to a committed family man, one of my sacred blessings. Our parenting styles are similar and we put a great deal of effort into our children. My husband and I, along with our three children, have built a solid foundation that works well for us.

My entire life revolves around what is best for my family. We operate as a family unit rather than two adults and three individual kids. Scheduling decisions are based on what is best for the family, not one person.

2) FREEDOM I have always lived by my own rules. As a kid, I would rebel against my dad's strict rules. As a professional employee, I valued the freedom to make decisions and not be micromanaged. However, it wasn't until I was laid off in teaching for a second time (due to budget cuts) that I understood how important freedom was to my happiness.

I was a professional steady-paycheck employee for 14 years. I highly valued the stability of knowing I could pay my bills no matter what was happening with the economy or the world. My whole first year as a 100% commissioned real estate broker I was sick to my stomach, learning to live with no safety net.

Years later, I cannot imagine going back to being an employee in a traditional system. As I have matured I have accepted that my passion, energy level and drive are dependent on freedom of choice. I would be willing to do just about any combination of jobs in order to remain independent. People who have known me my whole life have said they always knew my truest career personality would be—an entrepreneur. I didn't want to accept that until I let go of my fears and experienced it for myself.

I remember not being able to understand why anyone would go through the highs and lows of being an entrepreneur. At one time I didn't understand business risk takers either. It seemed so much easier to work for someone else. After being a full-time entrepreneur for a few years, I finally understood. I think the best explanation of an entrepreneur is:

Entrepreneurship
You do it because you are compelled
to live your life on your own terms

Freedom for me also encompasses the gratitude I feel to have been born female in the United States of America. I appreciate the ability to challenge myself as a professional woman, own my own business, be a mother and have unlimited choices. My thankfulness for this freedom makes it so easy to use the choices that are available to me in this country. Only in this country can you go from low-income housing to being a woman with a seven-figure income.

3) GROWTH   I did not value traditional education when I was growing up. To be honest, I found it boring. I was held back in first grade because we moved so many times and it was the era of the open school concept. If you did not want to learn you did not have to. I talked too much during class. At six years of age I decided I was stupid because I had to go to summer school and repeat first grade. I decided if I wasn't going to be smart then I'd better learn to socialize well.

At age 17 I learned that I loved pursuing personal and professional growth. That year, while taking a marketing class, I was elected state DECA president. I found something I was really good at. Mentors encouraged me and showed me there are talents beyond literal academic knowledge.

In May of my senior year of high school my marketing friends were getting scholarships. That was when it hit me. I may not have been naturally smart but I could work hard. From day one in college I had a grade point average goal of 3.2 that I obsessed over. By keeping my eye on my goal, I graduated from my undergraduate program in Marketing Education with honors in 4 years. I later earned my master's degree in education and graduated with a 4.0 grade point average. Unfortunately, I still did not feel smart. I was in my early 30s and a master-level teacher before I could tell people that I was held back in first grade. I finally realized that there was a totally different way to feel smart.

The great part about what I call a "street smart education" is that I can learn anything that interests me. Once I realized this I have learned more and developed tremendously by reading at least 60 books a year, attending seminars, taking courses, attending networking events, etc. This is such a value for me that I read a minimum of one hour a day and work on my goals daily.

You can see as you read through my detailed description of my top three values that they are authentic for me. They are how I breathe. Anyone who knows me would easily be able to identify these three.

Normally, I would not go into that much detail to explain a point. However, I did it because you don't know me as a coach and we have not had the chance to work together personally. By demonstrating my brand in personal detail throughout this guide, I hope it will help you understand what I am teaching and get to know me as a coach.

Building a Strong Personal Brand

Your unique Brand YOU should accurately reflect whom you are and what you have to offer. Everything that you do should build the image of your brand.

A Strong Personal Brand DOES

- Reflect who you are and what you believe in (core values).
- Differentiate you from the competition.
- Identify the benefits of your brand.
- Consistently deliver value to your customer.
- Build loyalty.
- Communicate effectively.
- Serve a need in the market place.
- Reflect your true lifestyle.

A Strong Personal Brand DOES NOT

- Present a negative image of competitors.
- Make you someone you are not.
- Make you an overnight success.
- Make up for poor quality.
- Occur without a plan and consistent management.
- Consist of all flash and no substance.
- Compete on price.
- Change too frequently and quickly.
- Make promises they can't keep.

This list is important for you to understand when building your own Brand YOU. These ideas are the foundation that you'll work from throughout this guide.

Getting Started

Now it's your turn. I'm going to lead you through five quick exercises that will help you begin to define who you are, which is the essence of building an effective Brand YOU. Here is a quick overview:

Exercise #1: Values—Brand YOU will stand the test of time only if it is based on your personal core values.

Exercise #2: Strengths—Brand YOU needs to be built around the strengths you bring to your specialty area.

Exercise #3: Talents—Your talents complement your strengths in creating a foundation for Brand YOU.

Exercise #4: Motivators—Building an effective Brand YOU requires energy and perseverance. The only way to maintain those over time is to understand what it is that truly motivates you. Brand YOU will have to be built on these motivations in order to last long term.

Exercise #5: Perceptions—Whether you are aware of it or not, you already have a brand image. Understanding how others perceive you can help inform your decisions about your strengths and talents, and what you may need to change so your image better matches how you want to be perceived.

Exercise 1: Values

List your top three values below, with number one being what you value most. If you want, feel free to brainstorm a longer list, then select the three values you think you live out daily.

Top Three Values

1) _____

2) _____

3) _____

Once you have identified your top three values you can check your accuracy pretty easily. Take a look at your schedule, behavior, comments, and actions. Do your top three values show through over and over again? If they don't, just go back and edit your top three values. Occasionally, when people start this work they naturally write down what they think they "should" value. It is ok to start this way, if the work is difficult for you, as long as you are committed to edit your list with your true feelings later.

Exercise 2: Strengths

Brand YOU should highlight your strengths. Can you imagine a physical product, such as a soft drink, calling attention to its negative traits? Coca Cola would never say, "Our product may cause cavities and leave an aftertaste, but it's refreshing!" Product branding focuses attention on the positive and minimizes the negative.

Your personal branding will do the same. It's time to be really honest with yourself and zero in on your true strengths. Below list the strengths that apply to your professional life.

My Strengths

1) _____ 7) _____

2) _____ 8) _____

3) _____ 9) _____

4) _____ 8) _____

5) _____ 10) _____

6) _____ 12) _____

Now go back and put an asterisk next to your top five most valuable strengths.

Exercise 3: Talents

The difference between strength and talent will be that you will have many more strengths. A talent is something truly special about you. It is what makes you unique. Talents are your unique gifts that you can share with the world. There are many baseball players who are good in the professional leagues, but Babe Ruth had a talent for hitting home runs. He was exceptional. Talents can be work related or not. Singing, sales ability, comedic timing, storytelling, patience, public speaking, empathy, etc., are all talents. A talent is a special ability you have and are a master at.

In this exercise, think about what you have to offer to the marketplace that is unique. Put some thought into the following three questions:

My Talents

1) What do you consider your best talents?

_____

_____

_____

2) Why do people like to work with you?

_____

_____

_____

3) What makes you good at what you do?

_____

_____

_____

Exercise 4: Motivators

Self-motivation is critical when it comes to personal branding. It does not matter if you have incredible strengths if you are not motivated to use them. Spend a few minutes capturing what really excites you. What would motivate you on a daily basis? What fires you up enough to work at it for the long run?

Here are two examples to illustrate the personal nature of motivators.

TJ's motivators	**Danni's motivators**
Giving back	Significance
Impacting society	Helping people
Discovering solutions	Recognition
Artistic expression	Positive challenges
A sense of accomplishment	Big paychecks

There will be no judgment for your answers. What motivates you? As long as it is legal and ethical it does not matter if anyone likes your answers.

My Motivators

1) _____   7) _____

2) _____   8) _____

3) _____   9) _____

4) _____   8) _____

5) _____   10) _____

6) _____   12) _____

When you have at least ten motivators on your list, go back and put an asterisk on your top three.

Exercise 5: Perceptions

What you think of yourself is important for the foundation of your personal brand, but what is more important is how people perceive your brand. So you are going to need to find out. The questions below are for your use in interviewing a few trusted people. You may want to ask people at work as well as your personal life. The key is to ask them the questions without making any comments. When they answer the question, write it down and thank them for their feedback. This way you are not swaying their perception.

Others' perceptions

How do I come across when I first meet people?

_____

_____

_____

What three words would you use to describe me?

_____

_____

_____

When you have the answers take some time to think about them. Do you like what they reflect? Do you have work to do to change a perception? No matter what your answer is, it will be helpful in creating Brand YOU.

Street Smart Lesson 1 Summary

- People–not just products or services–have a brand whether they are aware of it or not.
- Personal Branding (verb): a strategic process of marketing people and their careers as a brand. Personal branding controls the perception the marketplace has of:

1) Who you are.
2) What you do.
3) Your unique selling proposition (differentiation).
4) How you benefit your clients in your target market.

Personally Branded

- Everyone can benefit from personal branding.

- The elements of an effective personal brand are rooted in self-expression.

- Identify the values that are MOST IMPORTANT in your life. These will be the foundation of Brand YOU.

- Your unique Brand YOU should accurately reflect who you are and what you have to offer.

STREET SMART LESSON 2

What Makes a Personal Brand Great?

With any brand, personal or product, you have to look both at what image is created in the marketplace and what lies behind that image. Only then can you tell if a brand is great. Here, that means looking at both the characteristics of an effective Brand YOU and the person that brand represents.

As you go through these lists, you'll find that the assets that make a personal brand great are all what we call "soft skills" in business. Soft skills are personal traits, social graces, emotional intelligence, attitude, etc. Soft skills complement hard skills, which are the technical skills required to do a job. A simple example would be a doctor. Medical training would be an example of hard skills and bedside manner would be an example of soft skills.

For seven years, I worked for a superintendent who was a visionary. He focused on where education was going and what it could be, rather than the details of what was wrong at that time. He understood that educators are the school system's biggest assets.

He treated his staff as valuable resources and encouraged them to grow and improve. He also believed that schools are about building a community of learners. For these reasons he believed that the world could change in both education and business using soft skills to create connections and relationships. This employment experience taught me that soft skills are overlooked and underutilized. They offer the potential for major impact in personal brands.

In business there is so much emphasis on hard skills. Technical training is important, but no one would hire a computer programmer who was highly technical if he did not have the ability to communicate well or work as a team player.

In a survey given to human resource managers across all employment categories, 75% said they would hire for attitude before skill. The reason was that they felt they could train the skills needed for the job, but it is hard to change an attitude.

This emphasis on soft skills is great news because it means that every one of the aspects of a great personal brand can be yours for free! Here is a fantastic opportunity to greatly improve your business and you don't need money to do it.

Let's start by looking at the traits of a great personal brand, followed by the typical traits of a person capable of creating and sustaining a strong brand.

What Makes a Personal Brand Great?

Traits of a great personal brand

A great personal brand is:

1) Authentic
2) Consistent
3) Simple
4) Compelling/memorable
5) Credible

Brand Trait #1: Authentic

Above all else, great personal brands are WYSIWYG, pronounced "wizzywig," which means "What You See Is What You Get." You already know some people like this. Usually this term is used to describe someone who may be rough around the edges, but they tell you up front and honestly who they are.

Here it means that you are who you say you are, every time and in every situation. You are not trying to be someone you are not.

No one likes a faux brand. Great personal brands are built by people whose image matches their reality. People want a professional who truly cares about them and their needs.

People who have built authentic personal brands feel good about who they are and what they have to offer. They are the people who appear comfortable all the time. Authentic people are usually happier than people who are not self-expressed. Happier people attract more business.

BRAND-STORM: Name three very authentic people

_____

_____

_____

How will you know if your personal brand is authentic? **It reflects your true passion.**

People capable of building a great personal brand have passion. Have you ever noticed that people never become a brand cheerleader for a generic brand? They may like the brand or appreciate its value, but they never **LOVE** the generic brand. People love brands that have passion, especially personal brands.

Joel Osteen is a motivational preacher who created an incredible brand for his television ministry. Joel worked with his father at Lakewood Church for 17 years prior to his father's death.

When Joel was chosen to take over his father's church, he did not feel like he could do it. He had to learn quickly to honor his unique talents and let his style and passion come out. It's a lesson he learned well. One of the best things about Joel Osteen's brand is that he does honor his passion. He will even tell you he is not called to quote scriptures, tell biblical truths, or condemn sinners. He knows his best talent is to be an encourager.

Joel is an excellent motivational speaker. You can see and hear his passion each time he presents on television. Oftentimes, his voice cracks and a tear comes to his eye because he is so passionate about what he is doing. He has taken criticism for being too positive, too happy, smiling too much, and not quoting scriptures enough.

By honoring his passion, Joel has been able to encourage people to be their best, dream, and positively impact others. He is the number one television preacher because his brand is the epitome of passion.

BRAND-STORM: Passionate people

Who is the most passionate person you know? What do you like about them?

_____

_____

_____

Brand Trait #2: Consistent

Great brands reflect what people say they are, every time, in every place, which helps create raving fans. When you work with an interior designer you want to know that his work will be exceptional every time you use him. Furthermore, you want to know that he will give the same exceptional service every time you refer him to someone.

Do not underestimate the challenge of maintaining a consistent personal brand. As a human being you have emotions, physical challenges, and life events. You will not be able to be 100% consistent month after month, but your goal is to get as close to that as humanly possible.

For those of us with seasonal swings in our jobs, consistency applies on a year-round basis. Great brands are visible on a consistent basis.

BRAND-STORM: Brand consistency

List a few personal brands that you think show great consistency.

_____

_____

_____

Brand Trait #3: Simple

A great personal brand for you will have a simple, clear brand idea that gives prospects a correct impression of your unique selling proposition. That simple brand idea will differentiate you in the marketplace and attracts your ideal clients.

What Makes a Personal Brand Great?

Here are a few examples of independent professionals and their personal brand idea:

Permanent Beauty = Painless tattoos
Portraits By Christine = Tell your story with a personal portrait
Accidental Sales Coach = Contagious energy
Julie Clark's *The Safe Side* = Keeping kids safe from child predators

BRAND-STORM: Brand idea

Name four people in your community and identify their simple brand idea.

Brand Trait #4: Compelling and Memorable

Great personal brands are compelling and memorable to their target audience. The message is compelling or memorable because it is relevant. It may be serious, funny, or surprising depending on the product or service. It makes a strong connection between the prospect and the brand.

Visit www.kimandjason.com for a great example of this. Their mission is to help people escape adulthood and have more fun.

BRAND-STORM: Memorable brands

Name two compelling or memorable personal brands in your industry.

_____

_____

_____

Traits of the Person Behind a Great Brand

The people I've known who can create a personal brand that meets the criteria of a great personal brand are all:

    1) Confident

    2) Professional

    3) Committed

What Makes a Personal Brand Great?

4) Credible

5) Interactive

6) Responsive

7) Demonstrate high integrity

Personal Trait #1: Confident

Confidence is attractive. People by nature are pulled into confident brands. Confident personal brands give off positive energy that people want to be a part of. You can witness this at a party or networking event. Who do people flock to? Who is laughing and entertaining the crowd?

People want to work with someone who is confident they can handle the job and do it well. People with confident brands are often seen as the experts who will be able to overcome obstacles and achieve the desired results.

People with confident brands have a vision and conviction that makes them appear as though they are a leader in their industry.

BRAND-STORM: Confidence

Name two people who are very confident without being arrogant.

_____

_____

Confident brands also help the client feel more confident, calm, and comfortable because they know their needs will be met.

Personal Trait #2: Professional

Great personal brands handle themselves well. They always make what they do look easy and they do it in a positive manner. They have a level of class that matches their business perfectly. Their professionalism includes meeting the expectations of their clients, handling conflict and crisis well, and showing appreciation.

Professionalism does not always mean being serious. Jason Kotecki, creator of www.kimandjason.com, is a great example of this. Kim and Jason® is a specialty company that helps people escape adulthood through the use of cartoons, video clips, blogs, gifts, specialty items, and speaking engagements. He consistently promotes being a kid again. The company is fun, child-like entertainment, but they do it in a way that is tasteful and professional. You can see their professionalism throughout their website, customer service, and delivery system.
  Although the content is very casual and playful, Kim and Jason take the business very seriously.

Personal Trait #3: Committed

The truly great brands, both personal and product, have longevity. The simple explanation is that if a brand is not great it will not last long in the marketplace. Poor products and services fail in the marketplace sooner or later. People who are committed to

What Makes a Personal Brand Great?

staying in the game for the long haul reflect that commitment in their personal brand.

They show their commitment by doing "whatever it takes." Sometimes, showing commitment outside of business has even more impact. My daughter Katie accidentally threw her retainer out during lunch at school. I could tell by her scared voice on my voicemail that she needed help. Immediately, I went to school wearing white dress pants, shoes, and a sweater with feathers. When I arrived at school, the receptionist directed me to the custodian. His first comment was, "Oh, Sheri, it was tomato soup day!" I didn't understand. He explained that the kids do not like tomato soup and there would be a lot of red soup in the garbage that I would be going through. Determined to save the retainer, I climbed in the dumpster and, while standing in tomato soup, actually found my daughter's retainer. My daughter was very thankful and happy. End of story, or so I thought.

The following Monday I got a call from Rhonda, for whom I had done a listing appointment a few days prior. She promised to call to let me know if I was hired to sell her house. As it turned out, the school receptionist is Rhonda's mother and the custodian at the school is her brother. She said, "When they told me what you did to get the retainer back, I knew you were the right Realtor to sell our house." (My daughter accidently threw her retainer in the garage. I had to get in the dumpster and wade through tomato soup to find it.) Thankfully I was able to sell their house in six days and help them find a new one, avoiding a temporary move for them. They had big expectations and I did not want to let them down.

People with great brands also show they are committed by finishing what they started. People want to work with someone who won't quit when the job gets tough. Clients want to know they can count on you until the end.

BRAND-STORM: Exceptional commitment

Who exhibits exceptional commitment in your opinion?

___

___

___

What have you done to show exceptional commitment?

___

___

___

Personal Trait #4: Credible

Confidence… Professionalism… Responsiveness. All of this goes into creating someone with **credibility.** People with great personal brands have credibility to back up their marketing. Consumers believe that the brand (meaning the person) can deliver on what the image promises.

What Makes a Personal Brand Great?

Credibility may come in the form of experience, education, ability, or skill level. People with great brands have the credentials needed to make consumers feel confident in their abilities.

When a brand lacks credibility one of two things happen: either the brand fails or the person has to keep working until they earn credibility. People who have built great personal brands know what they are doing and make themselves look like a master while doing it.

BRAND-STORM: Credible people

Name someone who has great credibility and describe how he or she demonstrates it.

_____

_____

_____

Personal Trait #5: Interactive

Clients love to interact and connect with great brands and the people those brands represent. They want a two-way communication that is fulfilling to them. People actually buy a "feeling" more than the actual product or service.

People who maintain a great personal brand provide an experience and not just a product or service. The type of experience a prospect is looking for will vary but the fact that they want an *experience* from a great brand does not change. People don't go to

Personally Branded

a concert just to hear music. If that was what they wanted they would stay home and listen to a CD. They want the total musical experience that a concert brings. Someone may hire an interior designer to redecorate a room, but just as important is the experience they have with the designer, or the customer would just re-decorate the room themselves.

> **Exercise 6**: Becoming more interactive
>
> *Think about the ways in which you have interacted with your clients. What opportunities might you have missed? What could you do to become more interactive?*

Personal Trait #6: Responsive

People with great brands are responsive to client's needs. A responsive brand listens to the client, contemporary marketplace, and industry trends and gives their target audience what they want. An example of this would be McDonald's menu items. For decades McDonald's served popular food that consumers wanted, with little regard for health. It wasn't until 2006 that the children's menu offered apple slices with caramel dip. This responsiveness came from a number of influences in regard to obesity in this country. Several other healthy choices followed. McDonald's also phased out their supersize portions to help

What Makes a Personal Brand Great?

them move away from the link to obesity. This responsiveness has played an important role in McDonald's continued success.

In Wisconsin we have a high deer population and unfortunately, in the fall there are many car accidents involving deer. Car insurance can be a competitive industry. During a year of record deer accidents, an insurance company decided to remove their deductible for accidents involving deer. That may not seem like a big gesture until you learn how customers reacted. That insurance company had an increase in new business as a result of its responsiveness.

People respond positively to a brand that seems to care about them. People fall out of love with a brand that doesn't change to meet their needs.

Exercise 7: Becoming more responsive

Think back over the past 12 to 18 months. What needs have clients expressed that you have not responded to? Can you think of needs they may not have expressed that perhaps you could have met?

_____

_____

_____

_____

Personal Trait #7: Act with integrity

In the end, Martha Stewart and Stockbroker Bernard Madoff were not completely who we thought they were. When you find out a 13-year veteran referee of the NBA may be tied to mob activity and point shaving, you may change your mind about his brand. Each of these brands appeared to be one way in public, but was actually quite different privately.

Integrity is a very valuable commodity in business. People who are capable of building and sustaining great personal brands have integrity in everything they do. They are impeccable with their words and actions. They do not act differently when they are in the public eye. They honor their commitments. They do what they feel is right, even when it's hard or unpopular.

Their actions do not change dependent upon their bank account balance. If they have a high level of integrity, they will not bend the rules when business gets tough. Exceptional integrity means you would not notice any difference in brand delivery, whether the market was high or low.

When people can trust you to be who you say you are, that is an exceptional brand. Integrity is a differentiating characteristic in business, one that is highly sought after.

Conclusion

Were the 12 things that make a great personal brand what you thought they would be? Technical skill will always be important

What Makes a Personal Brand Great?

in any industry. That is an expectation people will have of you. Once the foundation for your industry is there, the rest is completely open for you to stand out. Take some time this week and think about how your personal brand currently compares to great brands. Let your creativity come out and brainstorm ways you can improve your brand to make it great. People with great brands enjoy their clients and that is reflective in their bank account.

Street Smart Lesson 2 Summary

- As with product brands, there are typical characteristics that make personal brands "great."

- Great personal brands are:

  1) Authentic

  2) Consistent

  3) Simple

  4) Compelling/memorable

  5) Credible

- People who are capable of creating and sustaining great personal brands are usually:

  1) Confident

  2) Professional

Personally Branded

3) Committed
4) Credible
5) Interactive
6) Responsive
7) Demonstrate high integrity

STREET SMART LESSON 3

Brand YOU Rules and Authenticity

Rules! Rules! Rules! Most adults hate rules. When we were teenagers we thought it was cool to defy the rules and do our own thing. Once you are an adult in business, that approach can be foolish in certain areas.

If you relax and let your rebel side think for a minute, you will listen to anything that will save you time or money in business. Smart people want to know where they can avoid a pitfall or wrong turn. One of my best coaching techniques is to help people stop wasting energy as a "right fighter" (being right no matter what). I teach the concept of "It just is." If they are going on and on about how unfair a particular policy at work is, I ask the client if they have any ability to change it. If they say no, then I explain the concept of "It just is." That is another way to help people see this as a fact. If there is really nothing you can do about a policy you are better off accepting it and putting your energy towards something productive.

So approach this lesson with an "It just is" mentality. After years of experience and research I know that the rules I'm about to share with you really are rules. They describe behaviors and approaches that are essential for getting the most out of Brand YOU. If you don't follow them, Brand YOU will suffer.

I've divided the rules into two sets:

> 1) The rules you need to follow when creating your personal brand.
>
> 2) The rules that will help you maintain and grow your personal brand over time.

Five Rules for Creating a Personal Brand

As the title implies, these rules should guide your decisions as you decide exactly what your personal brand should be.

> 1) Make sure your brand has value in the marketplace.
>
> 2) Put your best foot forward.
>
> 3) Align your professional and personal image.
>
> 4) Avoid faux personal brands and arrogance.
>
> 5) Create a good association for your brand.

Creation Rule #1: Make sure your brand has value in the marketplace

Don was a new Realtor. Several years ago he was one of my coaching clients. One day he gave me a call and wanted to meet about his new "branding" and get my opinion. Don was excited about his great, unique idea for personal branding. His idea was using an otter as his logo. He explained that the otter was fun and playful, etc. He really thought this would set him apart in the marketplace and people would want to choose a "fun" Realtor.

The problem with this idea for personal branding is that there are not enough prospects in the marketplace that would choose a Realtor based on fun. Selling, building, and buying a home is a serious financial and legal transaction. Customers want an expert. They do want to enjoy the process and have their Realtor make it as smooth as possible; however, most people don't want a fun-loving, otter-joking Realtor throughout the writing of their legal contracts. Sadly for Don, the perception in the marketplace was "who's this clown?"

After our conversation Don saw my point, and because he knows I care about him and his success, he took the feedback well.

About a month later, I saw Don's ad in a local realty magazine. It was beautifully done with great colors and graphics. It looked very professional, until I looked at the picture. There was Don in an expensive-looking suit, his dog by his side. When you are looking for a professional expert, such as a surgeon, would you go through the directory and choose the doctor posing with his dog?

The bottom line is that prospects want to know that you know what you're doing. In a situation like Don's, unless 90% or more of his ideal clients are pet lovers, I'd rethink the dog.

It is worth the investment of your time to thoroughly think through your branding to work out as many details as you can, before you rush to the marketplace. Carefully evaluate your brand before you launch it.

It is the same concept as the Super Bowl ads. There have been some fantastic advertisements that have created a good buzz. Sometimes despite the millions of dollars spent, consumers remember the commercial for its creative appeal, but not the brand name. In the end those companies spent the money to entertain people and win awards. The products have been valuable, but without strong brand recognition, viewers may unknowingly give other brand names credit for the great ad. To make matters worse, they buy the wrong product. Oops! Great advertising does not always mean results for the bottom line. If you want results you must spend your money on effective Brand YOU advertising.

There is a wonderful artist from Beaver Creek, Colorado who creates one-of-a-kind glass art. She prefers not to sell in volume because she enjoys the process of making each piece. For this reason, her art can be quite expensive. She knows that the people who have purchased her art receive amazing pleasure from her creations.

To add value she offers two concepts.

1. If a customer does not love her piece of art, she will buy it back from them within 30 days. This allows prospects to let go of the resistance to buying higher-end art. Customers can display it in their homes or offices without worrying about being able to return it if they don't like it. She gets multiple sales and very few returns.

2. She allows customers to send her small mementos that they want incorporated in their one-of-a-kind glass pieces. She receives everything from a piece of broken china to a feather. Her target audience loves this special opportunity.

Because she was clear about the value she offered, this artist put together an effective Brand YOU campaign, allowing her to work the way she enjoyed. She created a personal brand around her value that allowed her to stand out in a sea of talented artists.

Above all else, your brand has to be about something that has value in the marketplace or it won't be effective. Otherwise your money and time will be wasted.

Creation Rule #2: Put your best foot forward

You are going to tell the people what is great about working with you. You will certainly communicate this in a non-arrogant way.

You will be honest in everything you do. There is a difference between not calling attention to your mistakes and "socially spilling." Obviously, not calling attention to a mistake is to not say anything unless an apology is needed. "Socially spilling" is when you tell on yourself, usually out of discomfort, by bringing public attention to a mistake you've made. In the literal example, you spill a glass of wine at a party. You are embarrassed and say "Oh, my gosh, look what I did. I am so clumsy!" when instead you could have apologized to the host and asked how you can help fix the spill. An example of social spilling in a work setting is a comment such as, "Did you see I had a typo in the ad this week? I can't even get that right!"

The point is Brand YOU is to highlight your best talents and minimize your weaknesses. What you focus on expands as your competencies and comfort levels grow. We are going to focus on your positive attributes and they will get stronger and grow.

Creation Rule # 3: Align your professional and personal image

The best personal brands are built simultaneously with professional and personal alignment. Too many people make the mistake of not understanding this critical component of branding.

- If I am a favorite teacher whom high school students look up to and respect as a role model, I would not be supporting my brand if I were dancing drunk on a bar top in my community or in the newspaper for drunk driving.

- As a pediatrician, my brand would fall short if I scream at my children in the grocery store.

- If a friend finds that I'm frequently late or miss appointments, he or she would not respect me as a professional organizer.

Don't have the attitude that your personal life doesn't matter to your professional life. That is a huge mistake. Clients and potential clients lose respect for you when you do this. Live your brand through everything you do each day. Personal branding is not meant to be fake. Your brand must align seamlessly between your personal and professional life. If you are being your authentic self, that shouldn't be difficult.

Creation Rule #4: Avoid faux personal brands and arrogance

In home decor, theatre, and maybe fashion, faux can be cool. Some artists can trick your eye to see an aged brick wall or 3-D textures that are not really there. Some customers are happy having faux. They know it is not real and they accept it. They are happy to have the "look-alike" for a smaller price tag. There is nothing wrong with this. Faux, used in this regard, is openly admitted and accepted.

A personal brand built on all flash and no substance is not the way to do business. I'd better present my true financial situation if I want to sell to an affluent market. Talking about three vacation homes that I do not actually have will eventually blow up in my face. My level of impatience would eventually show if I only pretended to love children. You would notice if I presented myself as a car expert, but did not know an automobile brand you mentioned.

Over-inflated personas and arrogance are never cool in business. In the celebrity world it can be very profitable to create a persona people love to hate, a diva or drama king. In the business world this never works. It is a huge turn off. "It's all about me" marketing is one of the biggest mistakes people make in personal branding.

The old saying, "tell it like it is" is true in personal branding. Consumers will never fall in love with your brand if you are not who you claimed to be. Personal branding requires a high level of self-awareness. This may be very easy for you, or it could be difficult. Regardless, this self-clarification is the foundation of Brand YOU. To illustrate why, here is my own self-analysis of who I am when I "tell it like it is."

SHERI'S PERSONALITY/ATTITUDE

Sheri is:	Sheri is not:
Charismatic	Laid-back
Optimistic	Pessimistic
Resourceful	Shy
Warm	Cold
Personable	Reserved

Brand YOU Rules and Authenticity

Sheri is:	Sheri is not:
Compassionate	Reckless
Creative	Quitter
Giving	Greedy
Sassy	Meek
Ambitious	Quiet
High Expectations	Calm

Exercise #8: Tell it like it is

Use the form below to begin your own list. Try to be as honest as possible. This is not an exercise in judgment. You simply clarify and bring to your awareness who you are and who you are not.

PERSONALITY/ATTITUDE

I am:	I am not:

If you want a characteristic that you do not currently possess to be part of your brand, use your Brand YOU template (end of Lesson 4: Brand YOU Foundation) as a guide and practice until you feel comfortable with that characteristic. Building Brand YOU is a great way to work on skills or attributes that you want to strengthen. Like any smart businessperson, you work on it quietly to gain experience or acquire it until you naturally possess the skill or attribute. Then you can publicly use it in your Brand YOU promotion.

Creation Rule #5: Create a good association for Brand YOU

People love to be associated with a great brand. We are brand crazy in the USA. We wear labels like a banner of pride all over ourselves. There seems to be an obsession with clearly wearing a brand label to make a statement about who we are. UnderArmour shirts, Lucky jeans, Coach purses, Dolce & Gabbana bags, iPhones. We freely tattoo ourselves if we love the brand.

It might be unlikely that you create a craze to the scale of this brand-wearing phenomenon. But you do want to create a Brand YOU that people desire. If it is a great brand, people will want to let the public know that they are associated with you. You can make it fun and rewarding at the same time.

For example, my husband was a college basketball player. I am sure he will always love the game. He and some buddies like to play at a local recreation center. For years, they had a typical sports bar sponsor. Then one year the bar cut back on funding

Brand YOU Rules and Authenticity

teams and they were in need of a new sponsor. I said to my husband, "What about me sponsoring you guys?" His first reaction was, "Oh, you don't have to." We then had a discussion about how to handle business when you need a sponsor. He and the guys got themselves organized and approached me as a legitimate potential sponsor. I agreed to sponsor the team with one condition: they had to play to win or I didn't want my name associated with their team. The guys happily agreed.

I designed a high quality reversible tank top with a flaming ball hitting the hoop and SellBuildBuy.com arched above the ball. The guys had expected t-shirts. They were very pleased that my brand treated them like a real sports team. My kids and I attended every game. My husband appreciated the family time and absent sponsors lost out on opportunities. My nickname quickly became "The Boss" because the guys thought it was great to have a "female owner." We joked and had a lot of fun. They lived up to their end of the deal and kept winning. I supported them by going out for a bite to eat after each game. By the second year we were in the championship with no games lost! During that time there were a lot of close games, but the guys really cared about keeping their streak going. We all did. Before the championship game they brought out the large trophy. I immediately said, "I want that trophy!" The whole team was determined and sure enough, we won the championship! That trophy is proudly displayed in the sports bar at the SellBuildBuy.com office.

My dedication (part of Brand YOU) did not end there. To say thank you to the guys, I designed custom black, lined, wind jackets. Above the chest on the right chest a flaming ball embroidered with their name and "Champs." The back was a large embroidered brand logo advertising the SellBuildBuy.com website. A really smart woman (hint–it was me!) put her business phone number in white on the sleeve cuff of the drinking arm. The jacket was a recognition to them as champions and I did it in a way that continued to build on Brand YOU. From a personal brand promotion standpoint it was a unique idea; where else can I get 10 guys to wear a billboard for me on their back and get all that publicity for my website? It's something to think about; the back of a shirt or jacket has more readability and potential attention than a traditional location.

When your clients are proud to let people know they are working with you, this association is priceless to Brand YOU.

Five Rules for Managing a Personal Brand

Creating a great personal brand is only half the battle. Afterwards, you have to manage that brand carefully or it can lose its luster (and its business purpose). To ensure that your personal brand delivers, follow these five rules:

1) Be consistent.

2) Be the boss of your brand.

3) Turn up your own volume.

4) Don't let your brand get dirty or old.

5) Don't jump around with your brand.

Managing Rule #1: Be consistent

The number one rule in all branding is consistency! If customers have an absolutely amazing experience with your brand one time and are disappointed the next time, the brand will not be successful. It is true that you can't be perfect when there is a human component involved; however, you need to be as consistent as possible with every aspect of your business.

Branding a person is very different than a product or service. Consistency will help you present the smoothest possible image for your brand. The best way to do that is by having creative systems and specific routines. Having a written marketing plan with goals and target dates is a must in order to help you be consistent.

Managing Rule #2: Be the boss of your brand

You are the only brand manager for Brand YOU. You will have to step up and take the job seriously. As CEO, your most important job will be to act as chief marketing officer for Brand YOU. Regardless of the company or industry you are in, or if you report to someone, your job will be managing Brand YOU. This can be a fun job that you enjoy. The point here is for you to realize no one can do this for you. No one will be keeping you accountable to get your branding done. It requires personal accountability.

Self-motivation will be key to your own accountability. It's up to you how well you market your brand. Your results will have your name all over them. If you don't care, no one else will. When you do an excellent job of holding yourself accountable, you will be pleasantly surprised by the results.

Tammy is an independent sales professional. She committed to a full year of Brand YOU coaching and completed all aspects of developing her brand. Within 12 months she increased her revenue by 300%. Due to her hard work, she was able to continue on her own. From that point on she only used coaching for occasional Brand YOU check ups. Otherwise she held herself accountable.

One-on-one coaching like Tammy experienced isn't required to be successful. Often my clients decide to purchase Priceless Asset$! as a home-study guide. They have achieved similar results when they took responsibility as the boss and held themselves accountable.

Managing Rule #3: Turn up your own volume

This rule is a bit tricky. Throughout this guide, you are being told to listen to the client, market, and trends in your industry. This is all true and very relevant. There is just one caveat, though. Sometimes everyone else's opinion gets louder than your own. In this fast-paced world it can be easy to lose sight of yourself. An authentic Brand YOU means you can turn down everyone else's voice in order to hear your own. You need to hear *your* voice most clearly. What do *you* want to offer as a promotion? What would make *you* feel like you reached your goals for the year?

Brand YOU Rules and Authenticity

Your happiness is dependent on you being your true self. You will enjoy the process of Brand YOU if you approach it by paying attention to yourself. After you can clearly define your voice, you will position it so that it has value in the marketplace.

You deserve to feel good about yourself, enjoy your work, and do it in a style that works for you. I am a strong, ambitious, passionate woman and I am done apologizing for that.

Remember, that is what is so great about the jumbo box of distinct colors by Crayola Crayons®. **Stand up and be your best color:** almond, antique brass, apricot, aquamarine, asparagus, atomic tangerine, banana mania, beaver, bittersweet, black, blue, blue bell, blue green, blue violet, blush, brick red, brown, burnt orange, burnt sienna, cadet blue, canary, Caribbean green, carnation pink, cerise, cerulean, chestnut, cooper, cornflower, cotton candy, dandelion, denim, desert sand, eggplant, electric lime, fern, forest green, fuchsia, fuzzy wuzzy brown, gold, goldenrod, granny smith apple, gray, green, green yellow, hot magenta, inch worm, indigo, jazzberry jam, jungle green, laser lemon, lavender, macaroni and cheese, magenta, mahogany, manatee, mango tango, maroon, marvelous, melon, midnight blue, mountain meadow, navy blue, neon carrot, olive green, orange, orchid, outer space, outrageous orange, pacific blue, peach, periwinkle, piggy pink, pine green, pink flamingo, pink sherbet, plum, purple heart, purple mountain's majesty, purple pizzazz, radical red, raw sienna, razzle dazzle rose, razzmatazz, red, red orange, red violet, robin's egg blue, royal purple, salmon, scarlet, screamin green, sea green, sepia, shadow, shamrock, shocking pink, silver, sky blue, spring green, sunglow, sunset orange, tan, tickle me pink, timberwolf, tropical rain forest, tumbleweed, turquoise blue, unmellow yellow, violet, violet red, vivid tangerine, vivid violet, white, wild blue yonder, wild strawberry, wild watermelon, wisteria, yellow, yellow green, yellow orange. (can be cut down)

Give yourself permission to be your best color.

Exercise #9: Listening to your own voice

Some quiet time for reflection is important. Have a cup of coffee early in the morning, go for a long walk, sit in your favorite spot, or go canoeing. Pick the place that lets you relax the best. In these quiet moments you can drown out everyone else's voice. You will be able to hear yourself. Listen to just your own voice, not any others from your private or professional life.

Who do you want your role to be in the marketplace?

_____

_____

_____

_____

What do you think are your best skills to offer?

_____

_____

What is holding you back?

What are you afraid to do right now that might advance your career or social life?

You need to be able to say, "This is who I am and what I have to offer." When you are brave enough to turn up your own volume you will have clients who are attracted to you because of it. There will be other people who are not interested and that's fine. It's not personal. They just prefer something different.

Managing Rule #4: Don't let your brand get dirty or old

When you are in business it is critical to try and avoid any negative publicity that may adversely impact Brand YOU. As you know, you are the spokesperson for your brand and you need to represent it to your best ability. Let me give you a sensational example of a brand getting very dirty.

TrimSpa, an over-the-counter weight loss drug, was looking for a spokesperson who could boost sales. Anna Nicole Smith was a celebrity who at one time was Playmate of the Year, then years later found herself depressed and overweight. The CEO and founder of TrimSpa, Alex Goen, met Anna Nicole and liked her personality. She was at a point in her professional life when she was trying to re-invent herself; the legal battles with the other heirs of her late husband's multi-million dollar estate left her struggling financially. She was also having trouble getting work due to her weight.

A lucky break came when E! Entertainment launched a reality show based on her life. The first season of "The Anna Nicole Show" received high ratings and people were falling back in love with Anna Nicole. TrimSpa thought this was a perfect opportunity to make a name for themselves by publicly helping her lose weight. TrimSpa signed Anna Nicole as their spokesperson. She lost a remarkable 69 pounds (though some critics questioned whether Anna lost the weight solely because of taking TrimSpa).

Then Anna's image started getting tarnished. Her show was cancelled after the second season. She showed up at a major awards event, slurring her words and incoherent. During subsequent public appearances she seemed to be under the influence of something. TrimSpa's image was again questioned with her son's drug overdose and eventually Anna's.

These deaths are, of course, tragic events. I am not making any derogatory comments about their deaths. My point is not about the personal tragedy, but about the business decisions that were made regarding TrimSpa.

TrimSpa took a gamble on a spokesperson who ended up having a long-standing drug issue. Alex Goen may not have known about any drug use, or he knew and looked the other way to cash in on her popularity. I do not know what TrimSpa put in the contract in order to protect their image. It would have been a good idea to include a drug screen and continual monitoring for any drug use. When advertising for a weight-loss product, it's important to be able to prove no other weight loss product was used. In watching these news stories about Anna's alleged drug use, I remember wondering why TrimSpa did not pull her contract.

Ultimately, TrimSpa's name was left associated with illicit drug use and two tragic deaths. Now what? How do you save a brand after that? They spent eight months in damage control and subsequently launched a smart response. According to Alex Goen, they came up with the only campaign that made sense. Their first campaign launched with a white, crisp background to give a clean image, then before-and-after images of 200 real-life customers were used to demonstrate that the product really works. We will see if this new strategy will help TrimSpa recover.

The story here is dramatic to get your attention. It is your job to ensure that your brand does not get dirty. Examples of business dirt are being arrested, unethical behavior, illegal drug use, affairs at work, gossiping, negativity, scandal, backstabbing, fraudulent deals, laziness, covering up unethical behavior, etc.

Another form of business dirt is letting your brand get old. In order to continually engage your audience you will need to be on the cutting edge in your industry. There are two categories that you will need to monitor so they don't get old.

1) **Your knowledge in your industry.** This is critical. It is necessary to make a commitment to continually learn, in order to remain an expert. You can choose how you learn–seminars, reading, teleclasses, webinars, lectures, discussion groups, industry magazines, or formal classes. If you are passionate about your career you will be motivated to do this. If not, you have two choices: do it anyway or find a new career.

2) **Your Brand YOU campaign.** You cannot let your Brand YOU image or campaign get old. One of the biggest violations of this is when sales professionals never change their picture. It seems they choose the best picture they have ever taken, no matter how old it is. They are frozen in time. When you finally meet them you have to do a double take to see if it's is the same person. The sales professional always gives a nervous laugh and says something like "I know I need to update my picture." The funniest one I ever encountered was a real estate agent who had a picture on his business card with a suit and hairstyle that was clearly from the 1980s. He looked like a

young man just starting out. I was thinking maybe he had a different sense of style. He was dressed well, just not modern. When I met him at a closing he was bald. There is nothing wrong with bald; he just did not look like the picture on his business card. He sheepishly told me he had been using that picture for 15 years! A seminar presenter once said, "If you're scary looking, at least your business card warns them you are coming." It was a funny way of saying, "Be real. I want to know who you are."

Large companies keep a rapid pace of fresh campaigns to keep their clients interacting with their brand. You can update your personal campaigns at a more reasonable pace; however, you need to set up guidelines. Otherwise being busy will be more urgent than updating your marketing material. Setting personal marketing guidelines in advance makes it easy for you to follow through.

Example Brand YOU Marketing Guidelines

Marketing Item	Update Interval
Personal photo	Every 3 years
Refresh business cards	2 years
Update clothing	Seasonally
Change Voicemail	Every 14 days
Buy a new car	Every 5 years

The list could go on….

Personally Branded

Exercise #10: Creating your own marketing guidelines

Use the list above as a starting point to identify what marketing tactics you use. Enter that information into the table below. For each item, decide how often it should be updated, then note when it was last updated. When you've completed the Brand YOU work revisit the table, decide which items have to be updated, how the change should be made, and track the new updates. Once you have decided the frequency of each item on your list, you do not have to waste energy remaking the decision. You simply look at the checklist and schedule it on your calendar.

My Brand YOU Marketing Guidelines

Marketing Item	Ideal update frequency	Last Update	Current Update?

Managing Rule #5: Don't jump around with your brand

Call me old fashioned, but company hopping is bad for your brand. One of the main objectives of Brand YOU is to create trust and credibility. If you represent a particular company, clients trust you that the company you are with is best for them. I know situations change and, at times, professionals need to make employment changes. I also know Generation Y employees last about 18 months on average, so they may not believe in this old fashioned advice. Here's an example of the problem:

Dean was an office supply sales representative. He was active in the local Chamber of Commerce. Dean was also very outgoing and had a lot of fans. Every once in a while Dean would be missing in action at the Chamber meetings. People would ask where he was and no one knew. Before long Dean would show up again and announce that he was working for a hot new office supply company. Dean had a good personality so people were willing to overlook it. Over the next three years Dean seemed to change companies every couple of months. Each new company was described as better than the last and Dean would be off and selling again. By the fourth year people were avoiding Dean at meetings. Every once in a while you could hear someone say, "Where does Dean work now?" Eventually, Dean's hopping around burned bridges and he moved out of the area to find more business.

If people cannot keep track of the company you are with it makes it hard for them to trust your brand. Like the game of chess, you will need to make well thought out moves that keep the integrity of Brand YOU intact.

Conclusion

Developing and maintaining a personal Brand YOU takes work, but the steps aren't terribly difficult if you follow the simple rules in this lesson. You'll need to do some prep work to make sure that the brand you want to build will be valued in the workplace, that it emphasizes your strengths, and that it is accurate, both personally and professionally.

Creating the brand is only half the battle; *managing* what you create is equally, if not more, important. You have to make sure the brand stays fresh in the marketplace, and that *you*, not the marketplace, define exactly what the brand is and what it represents.

Street Smart Lesson 3 Summary

- This lesson described rules that will help you create and manage a powerful Brand YOU
- Rules for creating Brand YOU:

    1) Make sure your brand has value in the marketplace
    2) Put your best foot forward
    3) Align your professional and personal image
    4) Avoid faux personal brands and arrogance
    5) Create a good association for your brand

- Managing a brand over time:

    1) Be consistent
    2) Be the boss of your brand
    3) Turn up your own volume
    4) Don't let your brand get dirty or old
    5) Don't jump around with your brand

STREET SMART LESSON 4

Brand YOU Foundation

Abundant mentality does not refer to physical goods or possessions. It does not mean being obsessively materialistic and having an abundance of "stuff' in your life. What I am talking about is from your soul as a human being. You have an unlimited supply of smiles; you do not need to be stingy giving them to someone. You are not charged per day on the number of times you say thank you. Work does not have to be hard. You have a right to allow yourself to enjoy it. Mental abundance is free and unlimited. It means that anyone at any time can choose to be mentally abundant.

An excellent example of abundance is the word "wealthy." I can consider myself to be wealthy regardless of the balance in my bank account. I may think that I have a wealthy life because of good health, family, friends, a home I love, education, the sun rising, an affectionate pet, and a great attitude. Regardless of my financial status, I consider myself to be a very wealthy person. I am fortunate and very grateful for everything in my life.

If you believe you have to work hard to just get by, that is exactly what you'll create. Negative people tend to believe work is hard. Negative people attract conflict, repel people, and prevent good from coming into their lives. Limiting yourself stops the connection to abundance. Believing and acting as if there are unlimited possibilities opens your flow of energy. Most people are used to quitting after only trying once or twice. Abundant thinkers approach a challenge like a game and think creatively. How can I make this happen? At each dead end they hit they try another totally different approach until they get their desired result.

An abundant mentality is one of the best gifts that you can give yourself and your clients. Maybe you were fortunate to be raised in a family that understood this concept. People who live through an abundant mentality are optimistic, resourceful, supportive, not threatened by other's success, and live from a place of gratitude.

Scarcity mentality on the other hand creates negativity, competition, jealousy, judgment, complaining, and a constant feeling of lack. People who operate from a scarcity mentality are generally not as satisfied with their life as abundant thinkers.

We are so incredibly fortunate in the United States. We have freedom of choice. That alone can give you an abundant mentality. (I speak of the United States because I am an American and this is my experience.) You may be in a difficult situation right now or think that your financial picture is far from ideal. How you choose to perceive that will make all the difference in the world.

I am not a gambler, but given any circumstance, I will bet on the abundant thinker every time. We have countless stories of this being true in America. Chris Gardner, from *The Pursuit of Happyness*, is just one great story. If you ever think you can't achieve something, that movie will give you strength and amaze you.

People who use their talents to their fullest have a greater mission/purpose than money. Little green slips of paper will not magically do anything for you. It is really not as much about business as it is about elevating the spirit of others. Your gifts are completely abundant and meant to be shared freely. You will never run out. If more people understood this concept the world would be a much happier place.

At times when it is really tough in business and you feel like you have nothing to offer, try coming come from a place of abundance. Remember, you have an abundance of gifts to share. Do yourself a favor and use them. Too many people revert to poverty mentality and react negatively. Poverty mentality is thinking and reacting from a place of lack–limited resources, competition, and scarcity. Brand YOU would never come from poverty mentality. Can you imagine a salesperson saying, "I am the worst salesperson on my team, but are you OK working with me?" Abundant mentality would tell you that you always have choices. The game is never over until you quit trying.

Too many people are actually afraid to be as successful as they were meant to be. It's easy to settle, make excuses, and sabotage your success. To paraphrase Marianne Williamson's famous quote in *A Return to Love*, "You are not serving anyone by playing small." It's time to step up in life and fully participate. You have one opportunity during your lifetime to make a difference for the world. When you come from abundant mentality you don't hold yourself back. You know that you already have everything you need.

Come from an abundant mentality as you start to create Brand YOU.

Defining the brand comes first, and that's where we'll start. This lesson describes the personal foundations around which you can build Brand YOU; how to think about what you as an individual bring to the table. Defining this foundation is what will allow you to clearly, consistently define and express these four core questions:

1. Who you are.
2. What you as an individual have to offer the marketplace.
3. Why you chose to dedicate your life work to serving your target market.
4. Whom you serve (ideal client).

We'll start by walking through each of those four core questions, then use your answers to start your own foundation for Brand YOU.

Answering the Core Questions

Do you remember the rules for creating Brand YOU discussed in Street Smart Lesson 3?

- Putting your best foot forward

- Aligning your image

- Avoiding faux branding

The above rules are the reasons why you need to spend some time answering the core questions. The following work will help you clarify who you really are and what you want to be in the marketplace.

Core Question #1: Who you are?

Go back and review your answers to the first five exercises in which you defined your values, strengths, talents, motivators and what you thought about how others perceive you. Review Exercise 8 as well, in which you were asked to honestly define who you are and who you are not. Think about who you were as a younger person.

- What were you praised for by your parents or teachers?

- How were you perceived then?

- What were your favorite subjects in school?

- What extracurricular activities did you like best after school?

What other aspects of your background are important to who you are today and what work you want to do? Think about your education, past work history, volunteer activities, family, and so on.

Think about what your answers say about who you are as a person.

- How do you act out your core values?
- What really makes you happy?
- What do you really love?

Exercise 11: Describe yourself

After reflecting on these questions, write a short paragraph describing yourself as a person. What key aspects of your personality and behaviors do you think stand out to others?

_____

_____

_____

_____

Core Question #2: *What do you have to offer as an individual?*

One of the ways to define what you have to offer is to think about the attributes you bring to the workplace. Table A lists a number of attributes compiled from a research survey. They are highly prized by employers and customers.

Table A: Attributes Prized in the Workplace

Accomplished	Accountability	Ambition
Analytical	Assertiveness	Cheerfulness
Competence	Competitiveness	Cooperation
Creativity	Decisiveness	Dedication
Dependability	Initiative	Determination
Eagerness	Efficiency	Enthusiasm
Extroversion	Flexibility	Good attitude
Follow through	Good listener	Good natured
Helpfulness	Interest	Knowledgeable
Loyalty	Motivation	Organized
Patience	Professionalism	Speed
Quick thinking	Receptivity	Reliability
Responsibility	Economy	Skill
People skills	Strategist	Strength
Structure	Team player	Thoughtfulness
Versatility	Eloquence	Responsiveness
Accessibility	Honesty	Evenhandedness
Inventiveness	Perspective	Risk taking

| Visionary | Intelligence | High energy |
| Commitment | Integrity | Good communicator |

Exercise 12: Your attributes

Review the attributes in the preceding table. Use one color highlighter to mark each trait you currently possess. Then go back over the list again with a different color highlighter and mark the traits you would like to possess.

Looking over the above list, which skill sets stand out to you? Which three attributes are your favorite and make you want to build your brand on them?

1). _____

2). _____

3). _____

How could these attributes add value for your clients? The answer could be a valuable asset to your business.

Exercise 13: Map of attributes

If you are more visual, a mind map is a great tool to help you think about your best attributes and decide what you want to highlight.

The following example is from Bob Green, the athletic trainer, a name you may recognize.

Brand YOU Foundation

Put yourself in the brand circle and label the arrows by associations people have of you. Feel free to draw more arrows if that helps you. Do not edit your work at this stage; just fill the entire circle with identified associations.

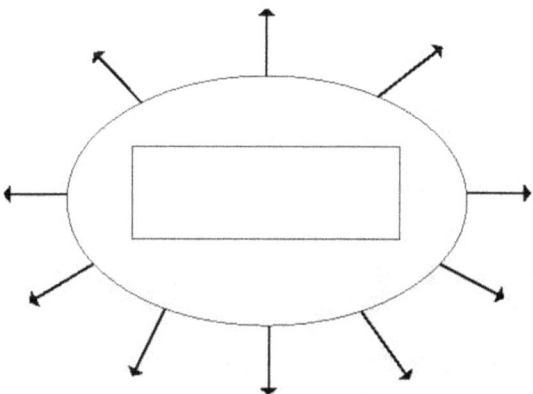

Now go back with your highlighter and mark the associations you want for your brand. You can see on the Bob Green example that I have put the highlighted items in bold. The items that you did not highlight will not be part of your brand. This makes a simple visual for you to start using.

Your mindset is one of your most powerful resources when it comes to the success of your brand. There are also three main areas that will shape your brand:

> The beliefs you have about yourself.
> 1) The ownership you have of your success.
> 2) Your attitude about your customers, products and industry.

Mental Programming

The beliefs that you have about yourself will definitely show in your brand. Both the conscious and unconscious beliefs that you hold affect the way you do business. If, in the privacy of your office, you are thinking:

"I am not worthy of earning more than $_____."
"When I get organized I can take on that new client."
"I'm too busy to _____."
"I looked like an idiot in front of _____. I hope I don't see her today."

You may first need to recognize these false beliefs. Think about what it says about you. Rationally you know negative self-talk is sabotage. Why would you play these games with yourself?

Once you recognize the underlying harmful belief, establish a new belief. The beliefs you have about yourself must support your success. An example of a new belief is, "I deserve to earn

Brand YOU Foundation

$_____ because of the excellent value I provide in the marketplace." You need to work on cementing this new belief into your mindset daily, until it becomes natural to you.

Exercise 14: Positive Mental Affirmations

Spend a few minutes thinking of some great affirmations for yourself. Examples are:

"I am very good at what I do and clients flock to me."

"I am meeting all of my goals and that feels fantastic."

"I am enjoying my work and am thankful that I make a difference."

Write at least 5 affirmations for yourself.

1). _____

2). _____

3). _____

4). _____

5). _____

What You Believe You Can Achieve!

Own Your Success

The most incredible athletes are the ones who take complete accountability for their losses and their successes. They are self-motivated and focused. In a positive light they are always self-analyzing the results they are getting and determining any adjustments they need to make to get the results they desire.

You can easily see how people get very different results when they take ownership for their success. When people blame others and make excuses as to why they do not have more success in their life, this is a big brand problem.

The bottom line is that you have whatever degree of success in your life based on how you have handled yourself. A personal brand that takes ownership of success with a healthy ego is very attractive.

Attitude is everything

Here's where the truth comes out. You may have a private attitude and a public attitude about your customers, products, or industry. If your true feelings are not positive and in alignment, this negative mindset will cause problems in your business.

An example of an attitude out of alignment is:

You work in a luxury business. You like the big payoff you get at this price point; however, you secretly envy your clients or think all wealthy people are not honest. Understandably, this incongruence will not work for long.

An example of an attitude in alignment is you work in a luxury business. You like the big payoff you get at this price point. You are motivated and impressed by your clients. You are grateful that you are able to be around and learn from wealthy, successful people.

Obviously, you need to believe in the products/services you are selling in the industry in which you work. If you don't, your brand has no integrity. Make sure that your attitudes about your customers, products, and industry are positive and in alignment with your brand.

Core Question #3: Why do you do your work?

This is your passion question. What drives you to do the particular work you do? Your easy answer may be to pay the bills. That is not a big enough reason to compel you to put your full effort into your work every day.

I used to answer this question with a small mentality. My "Why" was to help people live better lives and provide for my family. Remember, I came from low income housing so it was easy to think a decent life was shooting big. Then in a coaching session, my coach said to me, "Sheri you're playing too small. You will know your why is big enough when it goes beyond your life. When sharing your talents help to make the world a better place." For me, that meant raising the bar tremendously. For example,

- To inspire 20,000 people a month to use their talent.

- To donate $100,000 to education, $66,000 to reading programs each year.

- To donate $50,000 to women's advocacy programs each year.

That was going to take a lot of passion to make those contributions to the world. It compels me to get up every day and put my energy into everything I do.

My husband is a volunteer coach for several children's sports teams. When I asked him why he does the work of coaching he said, "It's so rewarding to see them getting better. It's a lot like teaching. I have talents that God gave me to share. It's exciting to watch them grow."

When I asked Chris, a chiropractor, why he does the work he does, he said, "It feels amazing to help people who are in pain to feel better so quickly."

Tim, a dentist said, "It's my family legacy. We have had three generations of dentists. I feel a need to carry on this rich tradition."

Brand YOU Foundation

Exercise 15: Why do you do the work you do?

List below your personal reasons for doing the work you do.

_____

_____

_____

Tagline for Brand YOU

Taglines are like a subtitle for a headline. They help you understand and remember the product. The best are pretty clever. Using two simple descriptors, the name of your company and tagline, you can have a way to communicate what you do to the public at large.

Technically, a tagline or slogan (the term is used interchangeably) is an easily remembered and frequently repeated phrase associated with an individual, organization, or commercial product typically used in marketing materials and advertising. The idea behind the concept is to create a memorable phrase that will sum up the tone and premise of a brand or product, or to reinforce the audience's memory of a product.

Some examples of taglines are listed below:

Company: T.G.I. Friday's
Tagline: In here it's always Friday.

Personally Branded

Company: Capital One Bank
Tagline: What's in your wallet?

Company: America West Airlines
Tagline: Low fare, fewer restrictions.

Company: SellBuildBuy.com
Tagline: A unique approach to real estate

Company: Street Smart Publishing
Tagline: Use Your Talents!

Remember, the point of a tagline is to have the marketplace remember your business and what you do. Listed below are some of the most influential taglines since 1948. Draw a line from each tagline to its product.

1) Got milk? (1993)   A. Energizer batteries
2) Don't leave home without it. (1975)   B. Timex
3) Just do it. (1988)   C. American Express
4) Takes a licking and keeps on ticking. (1956)   D. Las Vegas
5) Finger-lickin' good! (1952)   E. Wendy's
6) What happens here, stays here. (2002)   F. Alka Seltzer

7) I can't believe I ate the
whole thing. (1966)   G. Nike

8) It keeps going, and going,
and going. (1989)   H. KFC

9) Where's the beef? (1984)   I. California Milk Processor Board

Exercise 16: Your Brand YOU Slogan

Creating a tagline for your personal brand may seem easy because they should be brief; however, it takes some time and maybe quite a bit of brainstorming to come up with a winner.

My company: _____

My tagline: _____

Once you are happy with your tagline make sure that you check it against the criteria below. Is it:

- Clear?

- Consistent?

- Authentic?

- Memorable?

- Meaningful?

- Personable?

Now start using your tagline everywhere–voice mail, website, business cards, specialty promotion pieces, etc. These repetitions will help your target audience remember you.

Packaging: What Is Your Color?

You may have the freedom to choose colors for your personal brand, or you may have to use pre-established colors according to your employer. When you are able to choose your own colors it can be an advantage for you. With my marketing background, I have always been interested in psychology and color when it comes to advertising. The marketing research done about people's reaction to color is intriguing. One of the fun introductions I did when I met my new marketing students each year was to have them choose a color that best describes them. Then I would go around the room and tell each student about themselves, based on the color they picked. I would also ask their friends if what I said was true. The majority of the time the student and their friends agreed. For years the students couldn't figure out how I was doing this. My trick was in knowing the psychology behind the meaning of colors.

Each color elicits a feeling. Companies spend a fortune and endless hours creating their logo, building their brand and choosing colors. These large companies have conditioned the marketplace. Green pop cans make you think of what kind of pop (soda)? If a company with a new lemon-lime pop put it in a red can, they would be going against all the conditioning that has already taken place in the marketplace. What makes sense from a personal branding standpoint is to go with the general understanding of color in the marketplace and choose the color that best represents you.

I have two businesses. SellBuildBuy.com is a real estate brokerage. My color choice for that company was purely based on standing out, being fresh and looking unique. A strong purple with lime green was chosen because no one else was using these colors. Purple fits me perfectly. It's strong, bold, different but approachable. When I began Street Smart Publishing, I needed a distinct difference. My graphic designer and I agreed that we did not want to confuse people in regard to these very different businesses. Again, I needed a strong, bold, color that would stand out. Deep red with gold and bronze was the right choice. In real estate, I need to stand out and be approachable. As a presenter and coach, I need to stand out and be a strong person with expertise who can command a room.

The chart below summarizes a basic highlight of colors and their impact. Consult this chart when choosing your brand colors.

Color	Associated with	Preferred by
Red	fire, competition, heat, caution, optimism, passion	achievers, most secure, most economically stable

Color	Associated with	Preferred by
Orange	extroversion, adventure, celebration	adolescents, bright orange is second least favorite color
Yellow	sunshine, creativity, imagination, optimism, low prices, spirituality	the first color kids reach for, yet least favorite overall
Green	ecology, nature, balance, envy, spring	opinion leaders, trendsetters
Blue	dependability, water, sky, loyalty, patience, hope	#1 favorite color in America
Purple	passion, spirituality, art, creativity, wit, sensitivity, vanity, royalty	#3 favorite color, artists; loved or hated more than any other color
Pink	romance, sweetness, delicacy, tenderness, refinement, femininity	preferred by women or homosexual males
Brown	earth, substance, harmony, home, stability	practical people; down-to-earth people

Color	Associated with	Preferred by
Black	mystery, sophistication, simplicity, bad luck, night, power	intellectuals, rebels, fashion industry, increasingly broad appeal
Grey	neutrality, boredom, coolness, conservatism	not generally chosen as a favorite, usually not a big seller
White	purity, sterility, calm, mourning	intellectuals, modern types, limited appeal overall

If you have an interest in choosing the right color, you may want to do further research before you decide. If you don't want to spend so much time on it, go with colors you like and make them work for you.

Packaging: What is your "look"?

Just like a physical product your personal brand has packaging too. You need to consider how you want to physically present yourself to your target audience. Packaging your personal brand is about looking your best. It is not as much about how much you spend or brand name clothing, as it is about the **image** you project. You may prefer a calm, clean polished look. If you are a musician or artist you may want a stronger calling card.

I have always been an extreme balance person. I am all or nothing, black or white, going 100 miles per hour or asleep. I balance by doing the extreme opposites. In my professional life, I like to dress up in bold, unique clothing and jewelry. In my personal life, I prefer jeans or casual clothing. But no matter what I am wearing, I prefer diamonds and sparkly things. I shop at an upscale female boutique, Cache, because I prefer to wear things that you do not see everywhere else. I also shop at a discount store, Target, because I am value conscious and like Target's branding.

One of the funny things about this extreme difference in my clothing is that it helps me with my brand. I sell a lot of real estate in my neighborhood. I am very active with my neighbors, both as a neighbor and a Realtor. When I sell a neighbor's house we already know each other really well. The joke is when I show up casually dressed I am saying, "Now I am your neighbor." Any time I see them for business, I am professionally dressed, which says, "Now I am your Realtor." We laugh about it, but people can always tell what I am doing in the neighborhood based on how I am dressed.

Packaging, whether it is your clothing, hair, car or office, is a fun way to express your brand. Try having some fun experimenting with yours.

Presentation

How do you present yourself to people? This can have a major impact on Brand YOU. The way you talk, walk, sit, interact, eat, and drive can all add to or take away from Brand YOU.

Brand YOU Foundation

Something as simple as your manners at the table can cost you business. Do you slurp, smack, or slop when you are eating? You may not think so. Check with a friend for a second opinion. Every encounter in business is important. Present yourself as a professional and you will win.

Mission Statement

A mission statement is a strong, descriptive sentence or paragraph declaring your purpose in business. Your mission statement needs to be a correct reflection of your passion. You are not writing this to sound good to the pubic. This statement is an authentic reflection of your mission.

The Brand YOU Template

The kind of personal knowledge you've just clarified is critical in building a foundation for Brand YOU. I've developed a template to capture the essential information. Here are two examples of a Brand YOU Template:

Katherine Todd

Human Resource Consultant

Background

Katherine Todd has a diverse background. She has excellent experience in public relations, promotions, media, college relations, small business advisements and human resources. She has over

20 years experience with a vast variety of computer software. Katherine has been promoted ten times in her career. Hard work and dedication have paid off for Katherine and she is constantly learning and improving herself. Katherine is a very charming professional.

Brand Description

Katherine is accomplished, responsible and honest. She is professional, enthusiastic, and demonstrates follow-through in every task. Professional growth is important to her. Efficiency is her focus. People are never treated as an interruption. Katherine is a team player whom you want on your team.

Brand Slogan

"You can count on me!"

Key Attributes

Exceptional professionalism	Trusted follow through
Consistently conscientious	Confidential

Key Talents

Software and web expertise	Supervision
Budget with perfection	Trainer

Specialty

Ability to interact with people from all walks of life

Packaging

Katherine's style is contemporary without being trendy.

Her clothing, make-up and hair look very professional.

Presentation

- Professional, classy, and competent sum up Katherine's style.

- She is approachable and knowledgeable.

- Her written material is always professional and polished.

- Katherine has a warm, inviting personality.

Mission Statement

Putting integrity into everything I do.

Michael Fischer

Information Technology

Background

Michael has worked extremely hard the last three years to become a Microsoft Certified Systems Engineer. He has earned an MBA. He has been promoted five times during this time span, each time gaining more management responsibility. Michael completed several large projects recently, including:

1. Transitioning 150 employees through a corporate merger.
2. Serving as a key member of the succession planning board.
3. Assisting technical analysts in product progression for the end user.

He comes highly recommended by all who work with him. In addition to his technical background, Michael has eleven years of management experience.

Brand Description

Michael comes ready to deliver highly technical troubleshooting skills to large business accounts. He will work diligently to resolve any issue with customers in a timely, customer friendly manner. Michael is a strong anchor and brings valuable assets to his company's succession plan.

Brand Slogan

"Striving for progress"

Key Attributes

- Loyalty and team player

- Efficient solutions

- Total Quality Management is his style

Key Talents

- Exceptional people skills and technical aptitude

- Logically professional

- Firm, friendly and fair supervisor

- Top-notch trainer

- Web developer

Specialty

Exceptional Customer Service

Packaging

- Michael's style is traditional with high quality.

- He is always impeccably groomed.

- Michael wears strong, dark colors.

Presentation

- Michael's approach to every task is very straightforward.

- He leads by example.

- His confidence is apparent.

Mission Statement

Providing highly technical assistance with exceptional customer service.

As you can see, this synopsis provides a quick reference for themes and messages that Kathleen's and Michael's brands need to convey. It gives them a foundation for making decisions about how and when to communicate their brand that will be used in the next lesson.

Your Brand YOU Template

Now you have seen what a basic Brand YOU template looks like. It is your turn to create your own. You may want a trusted person or two to give you feedback on your first Brand YOU template. You will need to complete this exercise before you can move on to the next lesson.

Exercise 17: Completing your Brand YOU Template

Brand YOU Template

Your name:

Background:

Brand description:

Brand slogan:

Key attributes:

Key talents:

Specialty area/niche market:

Packaging themes:

Presentation:

Mission statement:

Conclusion

If you have done all of the exercises and Brand-Storms to this point, you have a solid foundation for Brand YOU. When you know who you are in business, that is a gift. You will find the more comfortable you are with yourself, the easier it is to do business. You will naturally know and interact with your ideal clients.

It is important that you only move on to the next lesson when you have completed all assignments through Lesson 4. Your foundation needs to be in place before you start creating Brand YOU for the public.

Street Smart Lesson 4 Summary

- An abundant mentality is one of the best gifts that you can give yourself and your clients.
- Scarcity mentality on the other hand creates negativity, competition, jealousy, judgment, and a constant feeling of lack.
- Core questions for the foundation of Brand YOU are:

  1) Who you are.
  2) What you, as an individual, have to offer the marketplace.
  3) Why you choose to dedicate your life work to serving your target market.

Brand YOU Foundation

- Three main areas that shape Brand YOU are

    1) Beliefs you have about yourself
    2) Own your own success
    3) Attitude is everything

- The Brand YOU template will help you clarify the foundation of who you are as a brand.

STREET SMART LESSON 5

Brand Management

Perception is essential in personal branding. You may clearly know who you are, but the key is how others perceive your brand. Brand YOU management is about consciously managing perceptions people have of you in order to sustain a powerful, authentic impression.

You are more likely to purchase or repurchase a brand you trust. A trusted brand has worked hard to establish and maintain that reputation. To make sure you are presenting a trustworthy brand it is necessary to continually manage it to maintain the best impression.

The following lesson is divided into three levels of brand management:

- Level 1: Basic entry-level Brand YOU management.

- Level 2: Routine management activities that need to take place on an ongoing basis.
- Level 3: Crisis management.

Level 1: Basic Management

These are basic tasks you need to manage Brand YOU. This section will give you a quick overview. I call them basic because they are easy to do and are necessary for personal branding whether you are a beginner or a seasoned brand. The basic management tasks are proactive success skills. The more consistent you are with these basic management tasks the more your brand will be worth.

Basic Management #1
Manage the first 30 seconds.

You have probably been told a thousand times that first impressions set the stage for the entire relationship. For this reason, it makes sense to carefully manage Brand YOU during the first 30 seconds when you meet anyone. Statistics show that 50% of people decide in three to five seconds if they like you. They may change their mind if they take the time to get to know you. That three to five second impression is human nature and vital to Brand YOU. Make the effort to be on your best behavior. Make sure you engage the other person. Use your manners. Listen. Be attentive. Look them in the eyes. Smile. It will have a major impact and be a low-cost activity for Brand YOU. Don't miss the opportunity.

Basic Management # 2
Don't spill—be careful about private information.

It's a good general practice not to spill your private issues in public. It makes smart business sense. Everyone does not need to know your private business. Every human being makes mistakes, has hard times, and has to deal with crisis occasionally. I am not asking you to hide in shame; however, you need to be cautious as to whom you tell.

The restaurant industry has a good physical way to explain this concept. They refer to the "front of the house," public area of the restaurant, and the "back of the house," areas that are off limits to the public. When you are working in the front of the house you are onstage with the public. The back of the house is for tasks that you do not want the public seeing, like the kitchen, manager's office, or supply room. The front of the house is neat and orderly. The back of the house may need to be messy at times. The door dividing the kitchen from the dining room is the physical place employees cross over from the back of the house to the front of the house. The door makes an easy reminder of the acceptable activities and verbal comments.

No matter what your professional career is, you have a front of the house and a back of the house. Your office may be the front of the house if you have to meet with clients there. If you do not meet with clients in your office it is a back of the house area. We all need places that can be public and private.

Make a decision to keep any less than brand-worthy comments and activities on the backside of the house.

Basic Management #3
Plan Sunday and the Night Before.

After researching the habits of successful people, one recurring habit was clear. Every day they make a commitment to plan ahead. Either the night before or early in the morning they plan the essential priorities of the day and write them down. Each of these successful people—from Mary Kay Ash to Bill Gates—uses this management technique. Many successful people also spend extended planning time on Sunday mapping out the week. When you plan by the day you only have a few hours. If you sit back and look at an entire week you have more time to pre-plan your priorities. This disciplined approach to planning keeps them from living in crisis management mode all day. Issues come up during the week that cause them to adjust their schedule, but it does not overwhelm them because the main roadmap is already in place, priorities first.

Basic Management # 4
Be focused and disciplined.

Entrepreneurs and leaders in business can have very different styles of getting things done. Business leaders tend to be held more accountable due to meeting the company's goals. Reporting to a board of directors, division heads, and supervisors requires business leaders to stay focused and disciplined. This doesn't mean it is easy, but *is* required to keep their job.

Focus and discipline are key to the management of Brand YOU regardless of which type of accountability (formal or informal).

Basic Management #5
Ask a better question.

Your first reaction to a situation sets the tone for how you will approach it. The majority of people have no formal training when it comes to asking questions. We just ask whatever comes to mind. A question is meant to seek further knowledge. A good question requires an answer that adds to an understanding.

Questions can be incredibly insightful and beneficial. I happen to love questions.

Questions that start with "What" or "How" are proactive and results oriented. Questions that begin with "Who," "Why," or "When" lack personal accountability and may appear to have a defeatist attitude.

"Why isn't anything working out right now?" is a terrible question. There is no accountability and it comes from a victim mentality. A better question would be: "What can I do right now to get things moving in the right direction toward my goals?" or "What would I do right now if I knew I couldn't fail?"

People also like to hide when they are dealing with questions. The familiar "I don't know" response can be frustrating. Sometimes the person may *not* know, but that just means they need to think about the question or situation in more depth. Other times, the "I don't know" response is a technique used to refuse to participate. Recently I learned a new reaction. When someone replies, "I don't know," you can say, "That is not very helpful." At that point you can either wait for a little bit to see if they want to respond (their response may be that they need more time or something totally different) or ask the question in a different way.

Remember, the point of a question is to seek further knowledge from yourself or others.

Basic Management # 6
Work on Your Weaknesses.

What experience in business makes you uncomfortable? What is your feeling regarding this experience? Where did it originate? How long ago did it start? How can you get past it?

Situations where you have made mistakes end up inhibiting you and keeping you from performing at your best. These weaknesses may vary from minor annoyances all the way to full-blown anxiety. Avoiding them can have a major impact on your business.

The situations in business that make you the most uncomfortable have the greatest potential for growth if you work on them. As adults, we enjoy doing the things we are good at. This is a natural tendency. We tend to lose the drive to learn how to do things we think are difficult.

Each week choose one of your weaknesses and sit down and work on it. Be grateful for your strengths, but work on your weaknesses.

Exercise 18: Working on a weakness

To start building the habit of working on weaknesses, pick one business situation that makes you feel uncomfortable or that you think you don't handle well. Brainstorm ways you could deal with this kind of situation differently the next time it occurs.

_____

_____

_____

Basic Management #7
Seek Growth.

In order to manage Brand YOU, you will need to continue to grow and evolve the brand. A personal brand that is working today will more than likely *not* meet the market's need in five years. You need to stay contemporary with the marketplace by continually evolving yourself and your brand.

It is much more comfortable to seek feedback that is positive and appeasing, but it doesn't help much. This is where a success group can be very helpful. For years I have been very committed to working with other business owners who continually seek improvement. We also push each other to be brave and move forward. This has been an invaluable group for me. You can do this casually or use a formal structure. My preference is the formal structure because it holds everyone more accountable. Visit StreetSmartPublishing.com and click on "Success Resources" for a free outline for "Running a Success Group."

Level 2: Routine Management

Routine management is tasks that need to be completed periodically. They may need to be done daily, weekly, monthly, or after each promotion. Just like maintaining any valuable asset such as a car or home, routine maintenance will keep Brand YOU in much better condition.

Routine management is also where most people have difficulty making time to get tasks done. The urgency of daily tasks may seem like a higher priority than your routine management tasks. Don't make that mistake. Schedule specific time in your calendar to get them done.

Routine Management # 1
Sit alone and analyze.
A very good coaching technique is to sit alone and analyze. Make a habit of going somewhere quiet. Write at the top of a piece of paper the topic you want to think about or the problem you need to address. Don't rush yourself. Relax and just make notes as thoughts come to you. Try to set your busy-paced life aside while you do this.

Sometimes ideas might just start flowing. Other times, it may take a few days for a solution to come to you. The more you practice this technique the more beneficial it will be for you. It is a way to train your brain to think differently. You identify a problem for your brain to work on and give it some time to figure it out.

You have to be committed to this approach because urgent matters always try to take your attention. Clients who use this technique have a scheduled time on their calendar and they protect it, such as the first Saturday of the month. Give it a try. It can reveal some very useful information that you might not otherwise have known.

Routine Management # 2
Sit back and coach yourself.

It is always more difficult to see your own situation clearly. One technique that may be helpful is removing the emotions. This technique helps you make clear, logical decisions.

If you were coaching yourself as a business owner or employee:

- What would you say?

- What can you see happening?

- Do you have suggestions that could help with the desired results?

- Is there something that this person needs to start or stop doing?

Exercise: 19 Coach yourself

Describe a situation that you are currently dealing with.

_____

_____

_____

Now sit back and look at the situation from a third party perspective. What do you notice? Can you see any solutions? What plan of action would you recommend next?

_____

_____

_____

Level 3: Crisis Management

Everyone will face various crises at certain points. No matter how good you are at what you do there will always be things that are beyond your control. The best proactive measure you can take is to have a crisis management plan.

I sort crises into different levels (ranging from 1 to 10, minor to disaster) based on the urgency, impact, and potential downside to my professional life. The better you get at correctly diagnosing what level a crisis is, the better you will be at handling it. Business people often misread crisis. Sometimes a small crisis may come up and people react like it is a life or death situation. I have seen a few managers who were at a level 10 and still thought they had time to slowly make their way through the issue. Other people

Brand Management

are addicted to chaos for the adrenaline rush it gives them. Living in crisis mode can ruin Brand YOU and may even shorten your life span.

The following are a few examples of what would qualify as a business crisis. You will need to be prepared to manage them in the best interest of Brand YOU. These crises are at a level 5 or higher.

- Risk management

- Lawsuits

- Information Technology
    - Cyber crimes
    - Computer virus
    - Damaging e-mails

- Business Cycles
    - Temporary cash flow problems
    - Surviving down markets

- Medical (that interferes with work for an extended period of time)
    - Long-term disability
    - Death of talented staff member

- Natural disasters

- Negative publicity that impacts your brand

Lower-level crisis would be anything that could affect the success of your professional life. You will more likely have to deal with this type of crisis. These crises are at a level five or below.

- Losing a major project

- Accidental errors resulting in major repercussions

- Company reputation
    – Damaged reputation
    – Marketing misrepresentation

What you always have complete control over is your perception and how you respond to a crisis. That knowledge should help you approach a crisis calmly and with an empowered mindset.

The following ten steps make up a simple, basic checklist to help you with crisis management.

Crisis Management Step # 1
Get centered.
The very first thing to do in a crisis is to get centered. You need to take a deep breath and relax. Focus on your business mission and get that purpose very clear in your mind. Vow to stay true to yourself as you approach the crisis.

When you are centered and calm you can make a better determination about the level of crisis you will be dealing with. By purposely taking time to pause before reacting you keep yourself out of "fly by the seat of your pants" mode. People who are addicted to chaos don't take this step. They react as if everything is a level ten crisis and run around getting high on the adrenaline. This is not how you want Brand YOU to be perceived.

Practice getting centered before dealing with each crisis. This is actually a great technique to start your day as well.

Crisis Management Step #2
Focus on the facts.
At this phase you need to focus on the rational versus the emotional. Clearly understanding the facts will allow you to make the best decisions. You need to go on a fact-finding mission and make sure that you clearly understand the crisis. Sometimes you will have to show a new perspective to clients. You may have to help clients separate emotion from fact. Once you have the facts in a crisis you can focus on priorities.

Crisis Management Step # 3
Focus on priorities.
During a crisis it isn't always easy to sort out what you need to deal with first. What is the overall goal when dealing with the crisis? Thinking through your priorities beforehand can help you remain focused.

When crisis occurs take the time to sit down and figure out your top priorities. Realistically, you may only be able to focus on your top one or two priorities. If you can do that, you should be able to make a plan of action that stays in line with your values and helps keep Brand YOU intact.

Crisis Management Step # 4
Make an action plan.

Proactively develop a plan that will resolve the crisis. Make a list of the critical steps you need to take and put them in logical order.

Assign each action item a deadline. Delegate if you need someone else to help take care of a particular action. Put your action plan on something that is easy to carry with you, i.e., your electronic calendar, a notebook, or clipboard. This will help you stick to the plan. Cross off or highlight each item as you accomplish it. This will give you a feeling of accomplishment and instill confidence.

Crisis Management Step #5
Have contingencies.

Plan A is always a nice idea. In reality though it is usually a version of plan A that resolves the crisis. I know you are probably saying, "I don't have time for contingency plans. I can hardly come up with plan A."

I know, but are you really going to risk putting all your bets on one option? It just takes a few more minutes to brainstorm other options for solving the problem.

Mrs. Fermanich: "What if that doesn't work out?"
Student: "Plan D is to work full-time for a year."

Spend some time coming up with plans A through D to solve your crisis. You may be annoyed with me at first, but when one of them works for you, you'll realize this advance planning was worth the time it took.

Crisis Management Step #6
Believe you will handle it.
The biggest courage booster during a crisis is to firmly believe that you can handle it. In the beginning if it's hard to get going, just keep repeating to yourself "I'll handle it." Before you make a tough phone call say, "I'll handle it." Before you lead a meeting say, "I'll handle it." Before you confront a situation say, "I'll handle it." This simple mantra sends a positive signal to your brain. Your brain believes it. This will help you start building success with the crisis and begin to turn things around. This is also a great technique to teach children.

A key attribute during a crisis is confidence. Be confident in your delivery and show the people involved that you know what you are doing. They, too, will believe that you will handle it.

Crisis Management Step #7
Be accountable.
This is the time to be really accountable. Do what you say you are going to do and when you are going to do it, then follow up. This is critical during a crisis.

Crisis Management Step #8
Communicate continuously.
A natural reaction during crisis is to hide and hope it goes away. How well does that work? It ends up making the situation much

worse. If we would just decide that we are going to communicate early and often we could reduce further problems.

Decide early on in a crisis that you need to keep clients updated. How often do they need to hear from you? Is it every hour, day, or week? It is amazing how much a crisis can be settled down just by giving someone information. This lets them know what is happening and what they can expect. Lack of information is just as damaging as misinformation during a crisis.

Crisis Management Step #9
Learn from your lessons.

If you pay attention you can see people who never learn their lesson. They keep making the same mistakes over and over again. Some even believe they have corrected the mistake only to realize later they are still making the same mistake, but in a different manner.

Then there are people who constantly try to learn from their mistakes so they don't repeat them. The military refers to this technique as debriefing. After every mission they sit down with all involved to discuss and capture on paper an evaluation of how the mission went.

A very valuable technique that I learned to use in coaching is what I call "What I learned." When I am finished with an event, campaign, or at year-end I title a piece of paper with "What I learned" written across the top. Then I evaluate what went well, what didn't, what I realized, and what I would do differently next time. This activity does not have to be reserved for negative outcomes. You can use it to capture your thoughts on successful results that you want to make sure you repeat.

This technique is another good thinking activity that can save you time and money in the future if you use the information.

Conclusion

Great brands do not maintain themselves. It is up to you to establish and maintain a trusted reputation. Good habits will be the key to making Brand YOU management easier.

After you finish this lesson, take some time to structure your work week and schedule the Brand YOU management success habits in your calendar. It will only take a few weeks to get in the habit of completing these management tasks and the payoff will be well worth it!

If you are anything like me, you will want to figure out how you can make Brand YOU management more fun. How can you celebrate when you maintain Brand YOU for a whole year? What can you do to make evaluation of each promotion seem like a game? Maybe you need a gold star when you complete routine tasks. If you are a more serious type, then figure out an Excel spreadsheet or calendar that tracks your results. The point is, Brand YOU needs to be your style of management to work.

Street Smart Lesson 5 Summary

- Brand YOU management is about consciously managing perceptions people have of you in order to create a powerful, authentic impression.

- To make sure you are presenting a trustworthy brand it is necessary to continually manage it to maintain the best impression.

- There are 3 phases of Brand YOU Management

    1) Level 1: Basic
    2) Level 2: Routine
    3) Level 3: Crisis

- Everyone will face various crises at certain points. The best proactive measure you can take is to have a crisis management plan.

- What you always have complete control over is your perception and how you respond to a crisis. That knowledge should help you approach a crisis calmly with an empowered mindset.

STREET SMART LESSON 6

If You Don't Brand Yourself Someone Else Will

In personal branding, it is extremely important to be able to laugh at yourself and learn lessons in business by watching the mistakes of other people.

I am an incredibly positive person and do not like to focus on the negative, however, a lot can be learned about personal branding by noticing what has negatively affected other people's brands.

Each person has a personal brand and may use it formally for business purposes or informally when meeting a stranger in a grocery store. Someone who is aware of personal branding and uses it to their advantage can make a dramatic difference in their life. This can be contrasted with someone else who is unaware of personal branding and accidentally gets "branded" by others.

In the following case studies I will share information about a few of my clients so that you can hopefully learn from their mistakes/

experience. Their identities have been changed just enough to protect them. The message in this lesson is: "Don't let yourself be accidentally branded. Get motivated to take charge of Brand YOU and use it to your advantage!"

Case Study #1: Sue's story

Sue was a high school physical education teacher who loved to have fun and had a positive attitude. Students and staff alike enjoyed talking with her. She participated in all the games with her students and related to them using their student culture. She was up-to-date on all the slang terms and used them jokingly to connect with her students. She was prom committee advisor and always helped with homecoming.

People always saw Sue laughing, talking, and using stickers and markers to make motivational posters. Without meaning to, Sue had created a brand for herself. Everyone loved Sue, but her brand became "Sue doesn't work very hard."

Staff and parents never saw Sue doing anything serious. She was always talking and connecting with people. One of her hangouts was the main office. The office staff loved her daily entertainment, but she constantly interrupted their work. Unfortunately Sue didn't realize she was causing a problem.

Over time Sue became frustrated because her male colleagues in the physical education department never took her seriously. They brushed her off and treated her like a student teacher even though she was 37 years old and had been teaching for 15 years.

She was convinced it was a "woman in a man's department" stereotyping.

To top this off, Sue wanted to be considered for a promotion into school administration. She made an appointment to meet with her principal to let him know about her new goal. The principal whom Sue respected a great deal, said, "I think you need to take a look at your relationship with the staff if you want to consider administration. You would be supervising the staff and they need to respect you."

Sue left the meeting surprised and disappointed, but still determined. She decided to hire a professional coach to help her determine what was wrong and to create a plan of action to correct it.

Sue didn't know about personal branding. She had to learn that "if you don't brand yourself someone else will."

Does Sue's Story Resonate?

We can all relate to Sue's story in some small way. Family members often brand us without meaning any harm. Some examples may include:

You're the black sheep of the family.
You're the last one to lend a hand.
You're obsessed with vanity.
Money burns a hole in your pocket.

Personally Branded

These comments may start innocently as your family's way of trying to change your behavior; however, you buy into it the more it is repeated to you. The "branding" may be true, but it may not be in your best interest because it is negative.

BRAND-STORM: You can't change what you don't acknowledge

Are you aware of any negative brand statements that you may have inherited? List them here.

_____
_____
_____
_____

You could get lucky—if you don't brand yourself, someone else could give you a *positive* brand. Have you heard things like:

- You never do anything wrong.

- You're the social director.

- Pam is so NICE.

- She's Little Miss Sunshine.

- He's so James Bond.

BRAND-STORM: Positives versus negative

Are there any positive brand statements that you inherited that you do not want? List them here.

_____
_____
_____

The problem is that even a positive brand given to you by someone else may not be how you want to be perceived. It may be a lot of undue pressure. "You never do anything wrong" can make you feel like you are not allowed to make mistakes. Martha Stewart is expected to have a PERFECT party, house, garden, and creative ideas. If you are labeled a "Martha Stewart," people may look down on you if you make a mistake. It may also prevent you from trying new things. In general, Martha has a positive brand image but there is also a group that looks negatively at the Martha brand. In order to show their disapproval of Martha's brand they make comments or even post cute signs saying, "Martha doesn't live here."

This is branding from the outside in: people telling you what your brand should be. What you want to do is brand yourself. You have to be willing to take the time necessary to determine what you are all about.

The great part about personal branding is that it can always change and evolve. If you realize you have been unfavorably branded—TAKE CHARGE!

Sue's Story, Part 2

During her coaching session, Sue realized what she was doing that made people brand her as "Sue doesn't work very hard." She wanted to make modifications to her appearance and behavior so she could change others' perceptions of her. We began with a short list of action tasks.

1) Sue's new brand–"Passionate Professional."

2) Only go to the main office for work related tasks and leave without chatting.

3) Tone down joking, especially in the staff lounge. (Don't be the staff clown.)

4) Post office hours on her office door. (Serious about work time.)

5) Always carry something with her, such as a notebook, book, calendar, etc. (Appear productive.)

6) Start making positive calls home to parents. (Be professional.)

7) Plan her workday the night before so she is more productive.

The following were the positive things about Sue's old brand that she chose to keep in her new brand "Passionate Professional":

1. High energy

2. Smiles for everyone she meets
3. Only positive talk and encouragement
4. Enjoys her students and has a passion for teaching

The difficulty for most people when adjusting a brand they have been given is to recognize that their old traits are not all bad. The qualities you perceive as negative could be positive if you modify them. For example, Sue's energy and passion just needed some minor adjustments. She would do a disservice to herself and the people around her if she suddenly was serious, quiet, and short with people.

Exercise 20: Brand correction action plan

Go back to any negative brand aspects that you listed above. Now you should be able to make an action plan for yourself modeled after Sue's example to correct these brand flaws.

_____

_____

_____

_____

_____

It will always be better to be proactive and deal with any brand issues as soon as they come up. Just remember that you are human and this is going to happen. If you are always putting your best effort forward people will be understanding.

Case Study #2: Ken

The following is a business example of what can happen when you don't take charge of how your personal brand comes across to the public.

Ken was a small retailer. His store was on a busy street in a small town. His business was open 7 days a week and Ken worked every day by himself. The name of Ken's business was good and so was his logo. He had already put two years of hard work into the business. Then, out of the blue, Ken sent his loyal customers an e-mail seeking financial help for his business. The e-mail basically said he was having financial difficulty and may need to close the store. He ended it by stating "If anyone can help, please let me know."

Of course, lots of people stepped up and joined the emotional cause of trying to save the small town store. One of my clients called me to see if I could help. I agreed to investigate by meeting with Ken to get a feel for what was going on. I spent a few weeks doing research and analyzing the situation.

There were some big problems with his branding of the store, but more importantly with his personal brand. He was not running the store from a business mentality at all. Ken had the mentality that as the leader he should be operating from his gut and not from the balance sheet. He felt that anyone with prudent business sense just did not understand his concept.

I gave Ken business advice and a marketing plan that could have made a difference. How Ken chose to implement some of those ideas was with a martyr campaign of "Save the Store." It became apparent that he was running a hobby shop and not a business. He would make comments like "sales are up X percent from last year." Ken did not understand that it did not matter what percentage sales were up, if his expenses were higher. It does not matter if informal surveys say people **LIKE** a particular widget. What widget people are actually **BUYING is what matters** if you want to remain open.

After a couple weeks I decided not to work with Ken. That may sound harsh, but my brand requires that I work with ready, willing, and able clients. Ken knew he was having problems a year prior. Given Ken's attitude, he was not ready, willing, or able to fix the problems.

The saddest part of this whole story is that Ken never understood his brand flaw. Emotional marketing will never last long. It is like quicksand. People are willing to help for a short period of time because they feel compelled to help. In the long run people will not do business or associate with unsuccessful brands. Ken could not recover from his brand flaws in this business venture. The bank closed the business two months later.

Exercise 21: What else?

Is there anything about Brand YOU that you need to explore further? Perhaps a flaw or two that could use some work. If so, what is it?

_____

_____

_____

Case Study #3: Terri

Terri is a female who was a high level employee who thought she worked well with her executive boss. She came to work being very professionally dressed. She had fantastic people skills. People genuinely liked Terri. She had an easy time getting clients and making large amounts of money for the company.

Terri had actually worked for this boss for five years before she started hearing comments from the office that really upset her. She is a very nice-looking person. She is in good shape and takes good care of herself. One of Terri's pet peeves is people commenting on her physical appearance and implying that work is easier for her because of her looks. Like most of us, Terri wanted to be good at what she did. Suddenly employees were hearing Terri's boss calling her "his trophy employee." We all know the connotation of a "trophy wife." Apparently, the term started out as a joke and then began to get more serious. Eventually, Terri started hearing it from different people, including Bob's secretary. Terri was shocked and hurt because she felt her brand was about exceptional results and ethics. She also thought Bob respected her intelligence and excellent work history. Terri felt she was not doing anything that would make somebody perceive her that way. She was prepared for all meetings, dressed very professionally, and always conducted herself ethically.

As an older gentleman, Bob, unfortunately got a sense of self-importance bragging to his male colleagues at Terri's expense. In this brand example, Terri needed to realize:

1) It was not fair.

2) This was not her brand.

3) Bob was probably not going to change what he was doing.

4) Her real job to correct her brand was to stay true to her style and brand.

One mistake people who get branded improperly by appearance can make is to do the exact opposite to subdue the image. It wouldn't help Terri one bit if she started dressing poorly or stopped showering every day.

Terri needs to be just as professional as she always was and not give in to this false branding. She should stay on her mission of working her flawless brand and do it with intelligence.

As a professional coach, I sat down with Terri and helped her see she wasn't doing anything wrong and that this was an unintentional situation. She could take charge and make sure to correct the situation because that is critical to Terry.

After some professional coaching Terri decided to take the high road. She had been working for the company for years, had excellent reviews, and was in a great position to be promoted. It was in her best interest to remain with her company.

In time, Bob retired. The situation actually died down without causing much damage to Terri's brand. It was unfortunate that she had to go through that ordeal.

Exercise 22: Identifying your accidental branding

Use the lists you created earlier in this lesson to compile a new list of everything you have been branded, positive or negative. Put an asterisk by the traits that you want to keep and a minus by the traits that you do not want as a part of Brand YOU.

_____

_____

_____

_____

_____

Conclusion

The point of this lesson is to motivate you to take a proactive approach to Brand YOU rather than finding yourself accidentally branded and also to show you that your brand needs to be continually monitored. You have already decided what your brand is, but what is it really? The real test is what other people say about your brand. You may have to do some investigating to figure out what the true situation is.

You may have to really heighten your awareness and refrain from any defensiveness in order to correctly analyze your brand. For example, you may think that people perceive you one way, but often they are thinking something different.

You will always be the manager of your brand. It is your job to be constantly paying attention and making small changes to make sure your brand is staying the way you want it to.

Instead of taking it totally seriously and stressing yourself, what if you just decided to have some fun with it? It's kind of like it when you were younger and first deciding what to wearing to work. You are picking out your external parts about your brand and also what you are sharing about your brand with the world, and sometimes that is fun.

Personally Branded

The takeaway lesson is do not, do not, do not let someone else who's branding you take charge. Make sure you are in the driver's seat on letting people know what your brand is.

There is nothing worse in business than being accidentally branded.

Street Smart Lesson 6 Summary

- One thing that is really critical in personal branding is that you are able to laugh at yourself and learn lessons in business by watching other people's mistakes.

- Everyone has a personal brand whether they use it formally in business or not. The difference is:

> People who are aware of personal branding and use it to their advantage
>
> Versus
>
> People who are unaware and accidentally get branded

- Brands given to you by someone else may not be how you want to be perceived by others. This is branding from the outside in: people telling you what your brand is.

- The great part about personal branding is that it can always change and evolve. If you realize you have been unfavorably branded – TAKE CHARGE!

- The difficulty for most people if they need to adjust a brand that they have been given is to recognize that their old traits are not all bad.

- It is always better to be proactive and deal with any brand issues right when they come up.

- It is not possible for personal brands to be perfect.

- The point of this chapter is to motivate you to take a proactive approach to Brand YOU rather than finding yourself accidentally branded.

STREET SMART LESSON 7

Courageously Live Brand YOU

Our deepest fear is not that we are inadequate. **Our deepest fear is that we are powerful beyond measure.** *It is our light, not our darkness that most frightens us. We ask ourselves, Who am I to be brilliant, gorgeous, talented, fabulous? Actually, who are you not to be? You are a child of God. Your playing small does not serve the world. There is nothing enlightened about shrinking so that other people won't feel insecure around you. We are all meant to shine, as children do. We were born to make manifest the glory of God that is within us. It's not just in some of us; It's in everyone. And as we let our own light shine, we unconsciously give other people permission to do the same. As we are liberated from our own fear, our presence automatically liberates others.*

Marianne Williamson – *A Return to Love*

People often say they think they have a fear of failure and/or fear of success.

If this quote is true for you and your deepest fear is that you are powerful beyond measure, think about what that says about you. What are you afraid of? What would be so scary about meeting all of your goals, maximizing your income, or being the best person you can be? Are you ready to be brave and totally take control?

Now that Brand YOU is solid in your mind it's time to jump off the cliff with no regrets. After all of this work you know who you are and how you want to be perceived. There is no more hiding. You need to get out in public and courageously live Brand YOU.

When you tune down everyone else's feedback and focus on hearing yourself you will do your best work. The only way you will maximize your brand is by being willing to go for it even if you have to walk alone. Top producers are always willing to walk alone when it is required. They have strong convictions about what they are doing and are not going to let others hold them back.

One of the biggest misconceptions about successful people is that they don't feel fear. I have heard so many people say, I'm not as brave as you are. That is what people tell themselves so they don't have to face their fears. The truth is that successful people do experience the same fears you do. Risk is not easier for them. They feel the same anxiety, queasy stomachs, and go weak in the knees, just as you do. Their secret is that they push through the fear and do it anyway. They do not let fear stop them. If the difference between you and greater success is learning to feel the fear and do it anyway, aren't you willing to challenge yourself a bit?

What if your need to control, deny, and avoid fear were actually holding you back?

Explore Risk

As you get older, you may think it's more difficult to take risks. If that's true for you, I suggest you use a symbolic metaphor for your risk.

Several years ago I was dealing with a challenge in my life. There were things I needed to do, but I didn't feel strong enough to courageously face them.

When I feel like that I know it's time to make myself risk a little bit to stretch myself. I decided to attend a Tony Robbins seminar, *Unleash the Power*, and learn to walk on burning coals. It does not matter if you like Tony Robbins or not. The point was I needed to make myself do something I did not believe I could do. There was no way I was leaving the seminar without successfully walking across the coals. I will be honest and say that there were times during the fire burning and heating up of the coals in the pitch dark of night that I thought I was crazy to be doing this. Again, it was just about facing my fears and walking my way through them. The other thing I knew from having gone through childbirth was never tell yourself you can't do something—or it's all over. So I followed the coal-walking directions intently. I got my mind to focus like a laser on a bull's-eye and I did it! Twice. (I am an over-achiever and I needed the second time to really let it sink in that I had accomplished it!)

After the seminar, with the confidence that I could handle anything that came my way, I dealt with my fears. Over time I was able to handle each situation and move on. It was well worth the time and effort to prepare myself to keep growing.

In 2007, when I was ready to release Priceless Asset$ and launch my first e-commerce website, I needed to practice risk taking again. A few weeks before this product was released I went to Mexico with seven women in my family. My cousin Jen wanted to go on an all-day tour that included snorkeling, cliff jumping, and swimming in an underground cave and a lagoon to the ocean.

Jumping off a cliff was not my idea of a good time, but Jen and I have always had a good time together. I decided to go with her. It turned out to be a great day to focus on risking and totally going for it. Jen and I agreed that when we jumped off the cliff we were going to totally let go and symbolically allow this to be our leap into the next phase in our life.

As I jumped off the 30-foot cliff I **HAD to** scream the minute my toes left the cliff. Jen screamed after she jumped and was in mid-air. We both laughed. It felt good to just let it all go. Everybody has his or her own style.

All day we felt stronger and stronger as we mastered each adventure.

I always say I take *smart* risks. I do not take dangerous risks for the pure thrill of doing something outrageous. I knew that thousands of other people have walked on burning coals and cliff jumped with these guides before me. These activities were safe if I followed directions, and yet they were out of my comfort zone enough to make me very uncomfortable.

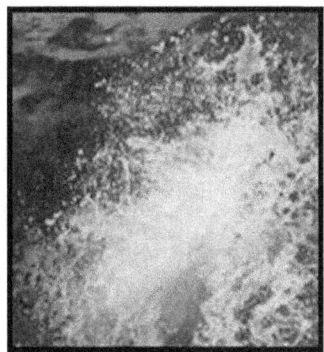

Embracing Business Risk

I am certainly not saying you need to walk on fire or jump off a cliff to fearlessly live your brand. What I am saying is that you need to transition fear from being the gatekeeper of your comfort zone to a resource that pushes you to grow. It's time to get out of your own way.

You can identify some of your business risks if you ask yourself daily questions such as: What would I do if knew I could not fail? What event have I not been comfortable attending, but if I had it would have advanced my business? Who am I afraid to call? What new skills do I need to develop? What's the worst that could happen?

The key to any answer to these questions is to do something right away to create movement.

FEAR is only False Evidence Appearing Real

You already know what roadblocks you use to try to keep yourself safe. They are the stories you tell yourself about why you can't do something or why it won't work. Lack of any necessary resource is another common roadblock. Thoughts such as, I don't have enough money, knowledge, self-esteem, or ability will keep you stuck. Whatever your roadblocks are you need to be willing to acknowledge them and learn how to work around them.

Exercise 23: Moving past your fears

List the most common ways you keep yourself from moving forward.

1). _____

2). _____

3). _____

Now spend a few minutes deciding what you are willing to do to walk around your self-imposed roadblocks. Don't move on until you have done this. You will only be cheating yourself.

Successful people continually make themselves stretch and take business risks that enable them to keep moving forward. They have learned to acknowledge, experience, and move through fear. Risk is not a four-letter word. Living within your comfort zone can kill your business, especially if you are in an industry that continually evolves or is affected by changing market conditions. You need to understand that not all risk will turn out the way you want. For example:

- There will be critics who don't like your ad.

- You will not get every client that you pursue.

- You can lose money on an investment.

- You could choose the wrong advertising medium.

None of these things will kill you. Top producers perceive these things as learning. They are in no way a personal reflection of themselves. Remember that fear comes from the uncertainty of not being in control. There is uncertainty everywhere. You might as well get use to it. Employees also experience the uncertainly of business these days. It is so much better to accept the fact that taking risks in business is a necessity and not an outrageous activity for thrill seekers. Start daring yourself more in your business life.

Playing the Risk Game

We are going to play a risk game for the next thirty days. We need to create an environment where you are focused on productivity and progressively showing yourself what you are capable of achieving.

As I mentioned earlier in this lesson, you will have your own style of approaching risk. You may be one who decides you are going to start small and work your way up to larger risks, or you may decide to do something big to get yourself started.

I never ask my clients to do anything I am not willing to do myself. When I first started playing the risk game, my style, as you might guess, was to do something big that was out of my comfort zone. I decided to have a "Secret" party. I was going to put myself out there and do a private showing of the DVD *The Secret*. It had just been featured on the Oprah show and now that everyone was talking about it. (I had gotten the DVD a year prior but had not talked about it publicly.) I thought about holding the party at my house. I had the space, but I didn't really want to do an open invitation into my private space with complete strangers. I decided to hold the party at a local restaurant where they let you show movies.

Then I asked a better question: "Where would be the perfect place to have this party?" I knew the answer right away. There is an amazing builders' parade home in a nearby town that is perfect. It's a million-dollar home with all the bells and whistles. The home is warm and inviting and has features that the average person would not have in their home. It also has a $50,000 home theater that has unbelievable seating that includes two column niches with a mural of our capital at night in the background. The closed doors to the theater reveal a library of bookcases as the backdrop of the bar. Two cylinder fireplaces flank the opening. This home was perfect. Now what?

I called the builder and explained my idea and asked if he would let me host the party at his parade home. Talk about guts. I couldn't believe it. But the setting was perfect and somehow I knew he would say yes. The builder was amazing about it. He openly welcomed this unique idea. His attitude about selling this house was "it's all about exposure." Wow! He could have easily said no way, but he didn't. The worst he could have said was no, because I was brave enough to go for it, he and I both were going to have an amazing experience.

I created an electronic invitation at evites.com. To practice the law of attraction (taught in *The Secret*) I decided to invite the first layer of guests and allow them to forward the invitation to anyone else they wanted to. We were not going to limit this fun opportunity. I even attached the data sheet for the house to the invitation. To add an element of fun to the event the guests were given a password to use at the door and asked to wear something that made a statement about who they are. I wanted them to know this was going to be an exciting event.

As a smart business move I invited the builder to attend and have his company literature available around the house. What a great opportunity for him to meet people he may never have met had he not been so open to new ideas.

I was thrilled all day when he said yes. I loved that house and for a night I would be able to create an incredible opportunity for so many people. It created such a buzz as people started telling other people about it. Now that's fun adult play.

As a result of the party I bought one home and sold another home for a total commission of $31,150, a doctor received two new patients, and a friend met a new boyfriend. As a bonus, James Ray's (a teacher in The Secret movie) personal trainer attended the party.

With just a little or a lot of risk you can grow into an amazing Brand YOU.

Exercise 24: 30 Risks

Think of 30 risks that you could take, one per day, and list them below. Then review the list and start to ask yourself:

What would I do if I knew I couldn't fail?

It may be a phone call to someone you have been wanting as a client. It may be to take on a project that felt out of your reach in the past. It may be to say no to something that is not ideal for your business. It may be to strive for the sales/business goal you were afraid to put in writing. Maybe it's time for new business cards showing your Brand YOU. Keep asking the question – "What would you do if you knew you couldn't fail?" Let your mind wander with the answers.

Review this list each day for the next month. Use your highlighter to indicate the risk you accomplished that day. (Using a highlighter as opposed to making a line to cross off an item helps you visually see how much you have done and positively reinforces your growth.)

30 Business Risks That Are Out of My Comfort Zone

1. _____

2. _____

3. _____

4. _____

5. _____

6. _____

7. _____

8. _____

9. _____

10. _____

11. _____

12. _____

13. _____

14. _____

15. _____

16. _____

17. _____

18. _____

19. _____

20. _____

21. _____

22. _____

23. _____

24. _____

25. _____

26. _____

27. _____

28. _____

29. _____

30. _____

Once you get into the mode of taking risks this kind of exercise is fun and amazing things will start to happen.

Having the Courage

Bravely showcasing Brand YOU to the world may take tremendous courage.

One of the saddest behaviors in our society is what is called "crabs in a barrel" mentality. You may have heard of this before. Apparently crabs will not let one of their own climb to the top of the barrel. If one crab gets ahead the others pull it down. In humans this may be negativity, jealousy, sabotage, comments like "who does she think she is?" or unethical competition. In fairness to yourself you need to be strong enough to ignore this behavior. Remember the quote that opened this lesson, "Your playing small does not serve the world." There is nothing enlightened about shrinking so that other people won't feel insecure around you. Someone in your family, a spouse, co-workers, or boss may be infected with crabs in a barrel mentality. You need to be able to ignore it 100% and stay focused.

Courageous Tips

1) Believe "I am good enough."

The number one underlying fear for everyone is "Am I good enough?" We all have our different hang ups and ways of expressing them, but it all comes down to this same basic fear. The easiest thing you can do to overcome this discomfort is to focus on the fact that you are good enough. Just because you are here right now on this earth you are good enough. You do not need to be perfect. The affirmation of "I am good enough" is critical every day, especially while you are taking risks.

2) Believe "I will handle it."

Develop a strong belief that no matter what comes your way you will handle it. When you have worries or doubt that can take a lot of your time and burn unnecessary energy. The calm affirmation of "I will handle it" gives you strength and confidence. If you get a message about a problem with a client, the first thing you should say to yourself is "I'll handle it." Denial and avoidance cause more stress and unproductive time then you can afford.

3) Use your passion

Passion is the fuel that will see you through. You need to let your passion for your business and goals be what drives you. Passion is a way to turn fear into excitement. Many times we mislabel excitement as fear when we're involved with a new experience. Focusing on why you want to take the risk helps you find the passion that you need to move forward. Keep your eye on the prize.

Risk Guidelines

For the past few years people have made comments about my risk-taking ability, such as, "I don't know how you do it." It wasn't until I realized how often people were saying things like that to me that I looked at what they were talking about. I did not consider myself to be a risk taker. I didn't leave my public school teaching career because I loved to take risks so much, or run my own real estate brokerage because I hope the real estate market changes so I can take some big risks.

To me risk taking is a matter of survival. I didn't have a choice when I got laid off and wasn't willing to work for someone else and put my three children in daycare. By the time I would have paid the daycare bill there would have been no money left. I **HAD** to make it work. Shortly after someone said, "That is how you do it. You put yourself in a situation in your mind that you have to make it happen. We see that as risk. You see that as essential." I had not realized that before. It's just how I handle my life.

After that conversation I sat down and thought about what I have learned in the last 20 years about taking risks. These guidelines I have found may make it easier for you to take a risk.

Risk Guideline 1: Only tell your dreams to and ask for feedback from positive people

This one seems like common sense but many people make the mistake of telling their dreams to dream killers. You won't get proper feedback if you tell dreams to pessimists. When someone has a negative reaction to something you are considering it is almost always more about that person's feelings about that risk than it is about your dream. When you choose to share with a negative person you are walking into a trap on purpose. It's understandable that you may really want a certain person in your life to support you, but the truth is they may not be able to support you. Be smart. Choose to share your dreams with positive people. A success partnership is a good place to routinely share your dreams. In a group like that people are prepared and conditioned to listen, encourage, support, and ask helpful questions.

Risk Guideline 2: Be willing to be open all the time

Being willing to be open means you can't control everything. You will miss chance meetings, unexpected twists, and adventures. You must have goals and a plan of action, but you need to be open to plans changing if something better comes your way. By going through your day with a spirit of openness you are more approachable. Be open to meeting new people, listening to new opportunities, hearing qualified feedback, and open to not always knowing all the details. By fearing the unknown you are giving up a lot.

Decide that you will go through your day more open to whatever may come your way. You can decide whether you want the opportunity or not when it shows up.

Risk Guideline 3: Practice evaluating risk quickly

Regular risk takers get very good at being open to risk and learning to evaluate it quickly so they can move on. I learned this great lesson on the first investment property my husband and I bought. I knew I wanted to be open to buying an investment property at some point. My husband was not really interested. He did not care if I was out learning and exploring investment properties, but he was not saying yes at that point. I read books and attended seminars. What I learned from these books was that you need to evaluate quickly or you miss opportunities. "Over-preparing" and "not going for it" bring the same result: either way you end up in neutral going nowhere.

Several months after I started looking, I found the perfect house. Because this would be a personal evaluation for our family I needed to get the emotion out of the evaluation so we could make a solid decision. I decided to use a one-page business plan on the investment property that included risks, rewards, numbers, and professional resources. After looking over the plan, my husband said "Let's do it." I didn't need to talk him into it because we were both able to see that this was a good investment for us. We purchased the house, added improvements, and gained equity of $54,000 in 18 months all while in a down real estate market.

Using evaluation techniques can help you tremendously in getting comfortable about taking risks. I have always known you can't put all of your investments in one category. For years I had been open to looking at any kind of passive income model. But when I first started evaluating passive income opportunities, it took me too long. Weeks were spent in the information gathering and comprehension mode. Now I can decide in a matter of an hour an opportunity fits what I am looking for.

Risk Guideline 4: Run the emotional evaluation, too

Every risk and decision is both rational and emotional. We are human and you are never going to be dealing with just the rational aspects in your life.

Here's a quick emotional evaluation that in conjunction with the rational evaluation above will help you make a better decision.

- Is it the right time in my life? (Losing weight following a family death may not be the best timing.)

- Is it with the right people? (The right decision with the wrong people can be a disaster)

- Is it for ME? ("Should" decisions don't last.)

- What does my gut say? (Learn to trust yourself – you are wise.)

You will make better decisions for Brand YOU if you start asking yourself these questions.

Risk Guideline 5: Only involve the necessary people

Too many so-called experts can ruin a good idea. Only involve the necessary people when you need feedback. Your aunt Betty Lou may be very opinioned, but unless she is in your target audience and can be unbiased you don't need her opinion. If you are in the habit of asking everyone you see for their opinion, you probably just end up more confused. By staying with the business decision to only involve necessary people you will make your risk evaluation easier.

Risk Guideline 6: Accept the fact the you will navigate and reach your goal like a pilot

Pilots know exactly where their target is. However, they are rarely 100% on track to meet their target. They are constantly assessing their situation and adjusting. We may think they are flying in a straight line, but it is actually a very jagged line due to conditions, etc. Your business path may also resemble a jagged line. When you accept that you will keep moving towards your goal but constantly missing it a bit, it will be easier to take the risks. You won't have the pressure of needing to be perfect with every maneuver.

Risk Guideline 7: Plan A, B, C, D

Get over the idea that there is just one solution. That is a big trap. While I was a high school marketing teacher I worked primarily with juniors and seniors. For several years I watched the seniors go through the stress of every adult asking them "What are you going to do with your life?" They were feeling so much pressure to make the one right decision.

This strange ritual, which happened every year, made me start thinking about how we teach people to plan. These students did not have a "Plan B." They were putting all their attention and effort into their "Plan A" and totally stressing out thinking that if "Plan A" did not work, their life would be over.

I would have been the last teacher to tell students that they could not achieve their dreams. In addition to supporting them, I always asked "What is your Plan B, Plan C, and Plan D?" Understandably they would get frustrated with my questions because they were struggling to come up with a "Plan A," let alone worry about more plans. Eventually they realized that by brainstorming more options they did not have so much pressure if "Plan A" did not work out.

The other benefit is if you have to come up with more than two plans you have probably really thought things thoroughly. Very often a student's "Plan D" was their best choice but they would never have come up with that plan in the first place had they not be urged to think beyond Plan A. Practice Plan A, B, C, D thinking and you might be impressed with the outcome.

Risk Guideline 8: Develop a risk management system

In each business there will be different risks that you need to manage, so it is not possible for me to give you a generic template. Develop your own system to manage any risk that you may have. Decide that you will make the time to put in place a solid risk management system for yourself. Areas that you may need to include in your system are:

- Education

- Preparation

- Assessment of risks and rewards

- Background checks

- Understand your product

- A power team

- Resources

- Reserves

- Limited liability

- Timing

- Boundaries as to when to walk away

Everyone would prefer a foolproof checklist of what to do every time they are going to take a business risks, but there is no such thing. Each time you will need to run through your own specific checklist. Learn from each evaluation and adjust your plan for next time.

The point here is to minimize your risks to Brand YOU by learning to manage them proactively.

Risk Guideline 9: Celebrate – Acknowledge yourself
Do you celebrate only if you win at taking a risk? It's time to change the way you are thinking! You will get stronger and be more willing to risk if you celebrate and acknowledge for any risk you take. The celebration does not have to be something big, but you do

need to take the time to acknowledge yourself and be proud of yourself for taking the risk. This helps you focus on the effort you are making to move toward your goal rather than punishing yourself for trying. The celebration should be something fun for you. It can be as simple as cranking the volume on your favorite song, eating cheesecake, or visiting your favorite place. The important thing is that you are re-training your brain in regard to success.

Risk Guideline 10: Have a recovery system

You are not going to win every time. Understanding this makes risk-taking easier. Realistically you win some and lose some. You do not have to take the losses personally. It may not have been possible to do anything better. So you don't feel bad about yourself when it does not go in your favor.

Here are five steps to help you recover more quickly from an unsuccessful risk.

1. **Acknowledge:** In all honesty, what happened? Take 100% accountability for to your role.

2. **Gratitude:** Learn to be thankful for the lesson that you learned and any good that came out of the situation.

3. **Forgive:** It is beneficial for you to forgive all parties involved. You and everyone else involved gave the best possible effort with what you had to work with at the time. Withholding forgiveness is a very negative, toxic energy that does not work in anyone's personal brand.

4. **Evaluate what you learned**: As described in Crisis Management Step 9 in Lesson 10, write a one-page

summary highlighting what you have learned. This allows you to analyze and take away good lessons that will help you in the future.

5. **Let it go:** Free yourself from any negativity and move forward.

The final phase of your recovery system is to figure out if this risk is critical to you and how to try again. You may need time, better support, education, a different strategy or motivation in order to try again.

Exercise 24: Facing your fears action steps

I want _____ *to and I scare myself by imagining*

_____.

Is this fear real? _____.

Am I ready to focus on what I want instead of what I'm afraid of? _____.

Make a commitment

I, _____ *, commit to courageously living my brand and allow everyone to see the real me. By doing this I will be able to make a bigger difference and reach my goals.*

I will start right now with my 30 risks list! _____

_____   _____
Your Signature   *Date*

Managing Brand YOU can be fun. It's not something that is going to happen on its own. You will need to take an active role. It can be a lot of fun to see what you can create by managing your brand well. Just like anything else, the best brand, left unmanaged, will eventually fail. A poor brand managed really well will still be a poor brand. You have the potential to have both: a good brand, well-managed.

Conclusion

To this point you have looked at Brand YOU from the inside out. You have worked very hard and done a lot of work that has focused on you getting results. If there is anything holding you back from fully expressing yourself as a brand, let me leave you this final thought.

What if you being the best Brand YOU possible meant you helped someone:

- Achieve a dream?

- Improve their life?

- Solve an important problem?

- Be happy?

- Connect with an important person?

- Change the direction of their life?

- Experience a difficulty peacefully?

What if Brand YOU was meant to make a difference in every life you touched? Don't you want to give that gift? What if the marketplace desperately needs Brand YOU?

I am certain that we do! You are the only person on this entire planet who can deliver your best Brand YOU. Share your gifts and talents so that the world can be an amazing place! Boldly express yourself in the marketplace.

Street Smart Lesson 7 Summary

- What are you afraid of? What would be so scary about meeting all of your goals, maximizing your income, or being the best person you can be?

- Top producers have strong convictions about what they are doing and are not going to let others hold them back.

- Successful people do experience the same fears you do. Risk is not easier for them. Their secret is that they push through the fear and do it anyway. They do not let fear stop them.

- **FEAR** is only False Evidence Appearing Real

- You already know what roadblocks you use to try to keep yourself safe.

- It is so much better to accept that fact that taking risks in business is a necessity. Start daring yourself more in your business life.

- Bravely showcasing Brand YOU to the world may take tremendous courage.

- Decide that you will go through your day more open to whatever comes your way. You can decide whether you want the opportunity or not when it shows up.

If you want to learn more about personal branding, remember to visit StreetSmartPublishing.com. There you will find a very comprehensive personal branding guide, Priceless Asset$, for entrepreneurs and independent sales professionals. You will also find numerous resources related to personal branding and professional coaching.

New teleclasses are offered each month.

Sheri is also available to give keynote speeches, as well as half-day and full-day training. Her schedule fills quickly so contact her as soon as possible you're your needs.

Use Your Talents!

www.ingramcontent.com/pod-product-compliance
Lightning Source LLC
Chambersburg PA
CBHW061508180526
45171CB00001B/93